MILLIONAIRE REPUBLICAN

MILLIONAIRE REPUBLICAN

Why Rich Republicans Get Rich—

And How You Can Too!

WAYNE ALLYN ROOT

JEREMY P. TARCHER/PENGUIN
a member of
Penguin Group (USA) Inc.
New York

JEREMY P. TARCHER/PENGUIN
Published by the Penguin Group
Penguin Group (USA) Inc., 375 Hudson Street, New York, New York 10014, USA • Penguin Group
(Canada), 90 Eglinton Avenue East, Suite 700, Toronto, Ontario M4P 2Y3, Canada (a division of Pearson
Penguin Canada Inc.) • Penguin Books Ltd, 80 Strand, London WC2R 0RL, England • Penguin Ireland,
25 St Stephen's Green, Dublin 2, Ireland (a division of Penguin Books Ltd) • Penguin Group (Australia),
250 Camberwell Road, Camberwell, Victoria 3124, Australia (a division of Pearson Australia Group Pty Ltd)
• Penguin Books India Pvt Ltd, 11 Community Centre, Panchsheel Park, New Delhi–110 017, India • Penguin
Group (NZ), Cnr Airborne and Rosedale Roads, Albany, Auckland 1310, New Zealand
(a division of Pearson New Zealand Ltd) • Penguin Books (South Africa) (Pty) Ltd,
24 Sturdee Avenue, Rosebank, Johannesburg 2196, South Africa

Penguin Books Ltd, Registered Offices:
80 Strand, London WC2R 0RL, England

Most Tarcher/Penguin books are available at special quantity discounts for bulk purchase
for sales promotions, premiums, fund-raising, and educational needs. Special books or book excerpts
also can be created to fit specific needs. For details, write Penguin Group (USA) Inc.
Special Markets, 375 Hudson Street, New York, NY 10014.

Library of Congress Cataloging-in-Publication Data

Root, Wayne Allyn.
Millionaire Republican : why rich Republicans get rich—and how you can too! / Wayne Allyn Root.
p.   cm.
ISBN 1-58542-430-7
1. Money—Psychological aspects.   2. Millionaires—Psychology.   3. Entrepreneurship—
Psychological aspects.   4. Capitalists and financiers—Psychology.   5. Wealth—Psychological aspects.
6. Rich people—Psychology.   I. Title.

HG222.3.R66   2005   2005049681
332.024'01—dc22

Printed in the United States of America
3   5   7   9   10   8   6   4

While the author has made every effort to provide accurate telephone numbers and Internet addresses
at the time of publication, neither the publisher nor the author assumes any responsibility for errors,
or for changes that occur after publication. Further, the publisher does not have any control over
and does not assume any responsibility for author or third-party websites or their content.

This publication is designed to provide accurate and authoritative information in regard to the subject
matter covered. It is sold with the understanding that the publisher is not engaged in rendering legal,
accounting or other professional services. If you require legal advice or other expert assistance,
you should seek the services of a competent professional.

Millionaire Republican is dedicated to:

My parents in heaven, David and Stella Root, who gave me my foundation in life.

Most important, my father, David, the Republican butcher from Brownsville, Brooklyn, who taught me the Republican secrets of success.

My grandmother Meta Reis, who taught me the meaning of courage and chutzpah.

My grandfather Simon Reis, who taught me the value of entrepreneurship and salesmanship.

My wife, Debra, and children Dakota, Hudson, and Remington Reagan, who teach me the meaning of love every single day.

My best friend, mentor, and loyal business partner, Douglas Miller, who has stood by my side through thick and thin for almost a quarter of a century.

My beloved Republican Party—it is your principles, rules, and values that fueled my success.

And most important, to God, who inspired my words and ideas, and to whom I dedicate my life!

Contents

MILLIONAIRE REPUBLICAN

Introduction: Rich Republican Dad, Poor Democrat Dad!

That some should be rich, shows that others may become rich.

—ABRAHAM LINCOLN

I recently read the blockbuster book *Rich Dad, Poor Dad* by Robert T. Kiyosaki. I loved it! One of the best-selling books of modern times, it stayed atop the *New York Times* best-seller list for a record 320 weeks! It has been praised as an empowering book—specifically for teaching young adults about how to think differently (i.e., more successfully) about money and building wealth. *Rich Dad, Poor Dad* helps explain the mystery of why some Americans are so successful at building wealth, while most are not. But as much as I loved the book, there's a huge flaw that Kiyosaki fails to admit or address. Undoubtedly afraid to add controversy to his message, he failed to use the more accurate title: *Rich Republican Dad, Poor Democrat Dad*. The book is the story of two very different fathers, their contrasting views about money and wealth, and how their lives turned out as a result. Those two dads serve to perfectly illustrate the dramatic difference in thinking between Republicans and Democrats about wealth, success, and career. Kiyosaki's "Poor Dad," his birth father, is a classic example of a stereotypical Liberal Democrat. He is a negative thinker who is forever down on his luck, down on capitalism, down on the opportunities available for average Americans. He believes life is unfair and that luck often helps to determine success. He is a strong believer that only through education and "book smarts" can you succeed. Yet he is angry that all his education and advanced degrees have left him financially insecure. He is not passionate about his career—to him, it's only a job. He is fearful and timid in his career, his investments, his life. He would never take a daring risk to start his own business—instead he craves what he calls a "safe job" and the guaranteed weekly paycheck that comes with it. He has spent his career working first for government, then as an educator—two professions filled with liberal career bureaucrats. He has no confidence in his own ability and looks to Big Brother to save him—whether it be a big corporate boss, a union boss, or a government boss. "Poor Dad" believes in big government and wants to "soak the rich," primarily because he never expects to become one of them. Not surprisingly, the result of this kind of mind-set is that "Poor Dad" is forever struggling financially and, after many years of breaking his back, has never accumulated any significant assets.

On the other hand, Kiyosaki's "Rich Dad," the man Kiyosaki adopted as his father, is a classic Republican. He is the exact *oppo-*

site of "Poor Dad" in every way. He is a positive thinker. He believes in himself and has supreme confidence in his ideas. Just as
all Millionaire Republicans do. He believes in America and the
ability for everyone to achieve "The American Dream." He sees
opportunity everywhere—in every deal, around every corner.
Just as all Millionaire Republicans do. He has no formal education or fancy degrees, but he makes up for a lack of "book
smarts" with a megadose of "street smarts." He is a daring, bold,
aggressive risk-taker. His middle name should be "chutzpah"
(Yiddish for *balls*)! He would *never* settle for a paycheck and a safe
job. He is constantly willing to risk his own money on his many
businesses and entrepreneurial ideas—just as all Millionaire
Republicans do. Since he doesn't see his job only as a way to
earn a paycheck, he doesn't limit his working hours to between
9 and 5. Like all entrepreneurial Millionaire Republicans, "Rich
Dad" loves his career, and as a result he is willing to work 24/7,
even on weekends and holidays. After all, when it's *your* business
it's not just a job—you feel as if you yourself gave birth, it's your
child, your lifeblood. Millionaire Republicans invest in the future of their businesses, the same way you would invest in the
future of your child. They think like *owners*, not renters. "Rich
Dad" doesn't believe in luck. He knows that all entrepreneurs
experience luck—and it's usually bad. That's okay. Millionaire
Republicans have a unique mind-set. They are fearless and positive in the face of failure, rejection, challenge, and bad luck.
"Rich Dad" doesn't depend on government. To the contrary,
he believes success is dependent on getting government out of

the way and knows that getting rich is all about limited government and lower taxes. "Rich Dad" is disdainful of the education system and what is taught in our schools. He knows that the teachers, educators, and administrators who are educating our kids may know their ABCs and the three Rs, but they know virtually nothing about money, wealth, or success. It's not that they're bad people. To the contrary, they are well-meaning professionals who care about their students. But you can't teach what you don't know. The vast majority of educators graduated from college and immediately started collecting a safe, steady (but mediocre) paycheck from a large bureaucracy—it's all they know. Educators and education bureaucrats have never taken a risk, never built or owned a business, never achieved the American Dream, and therefore never built any wealth or assets! And therefore "Rich Dad" knows that it is no surprise that these same people, who have little understanding of wealth or how to acquire it (and are actually uncomfortable with money and business), are teaching our kids to settle for a mediocre paycheck and a "safe job." After all, that's all they know *themselves.*

Author Kiyosaki is right on the money (pun intended) describing the difference in mind-set, attitude, and levels of achievement between "Rich Dad" and "Poor Dad." The only problem is that he forgot to tell his readers that "Rich Dad" is a classic Millionaire Republican, whose positive attitude, fearless risk-taking, understanding of wealth, unbridled passion for money, desire for financial freedom, and *limitless* thinking have made him wealthy and successful beyond his wildest dreams. And that "Poor Dad" is a classic Liberal Democrat, whose *negative* thinking about wealth and opportunity, and willingness to settle for the "security" of a mediocre job and a guaranteed paycheck from a large, faceless bureaucracy have limited his success in life and left him sad, depressed, jealous, bitter, and broke. Kiyosaki does correctly stress that the way you think will affect every day of your life. It will determine whether you wind up a winner or loser, owner or renter, thriver or survivor, successful and wealthy, or hopeless, helpless, and clueless. What he is afraid to tell you (or perhaps just too diplomatic) is that how you think will determine whether you'll be a Millionaire Republican or a poor, struggling, bitter Democrat. It's all determined by attitude and mind-set. But you can't change your attitude and mind-set until someone tells you the raw truth and provides you a framework for change. Until someone teaches you the 18 Republican Secrets of Mega-Wealth and Unlimited Success!

Now, before we go any further, let me tell you what this book is *not*. It is *not* a book about politics. You may disagree with the Republican Party on issues like abortion, gay rights, stem-cell research, affirmative action, the environment, the death penalty, or the war on terrorism. I certainly have my own opinions about many of those issues, and they don't always agree with the GOP party line. Who cares? This book is about one thing and one thing only. *Acquiring wealth.* It's about becoming a part of the "ownership society." Plain and simple: It's about *money.* The media elite and liberal politicians claim that the Republican Party represents the rich. Well, they're right. Republicans *are* richer than Democrats. The vast majority of millionaires *are* Republican—that's a fact. And do you know why? It's because we possess the knowledge of how to attain wealth and ownership—from our homes to our businesses to our futures. We choose to *own,* not rent. We understand that if you own, you are in control. Ownership and knowledge are power. We have both. Republicans have it, you don't. When it comes to money, there is no choice. You either think like a Republican and learn the Republican Rules, or you get *left* behind (pun intended). It's time to start thinking differently about wealth—no matter what your party affiliation—because you can't afford to be closed-minded.

The Republican Party is the party of success. It is the party of *ownership.* If you want to achieve success, acquire wealth, accumulate assets, take control of your future—*own instead of rent your life*—you had better base your "model" of success on rich Republicans. In this book, I'm going to share with you the knowledge of how to become part of the ownership society—the knowledge of how to become a Millionaire Republican.

How do I know so much about wealth? It's not because I've studied it in a book. It's because I've lived it! My name is Wayne Allyn Root and I am a Millionaire Republican. That's not a confession—although any politically correct liberals who are reading this are probably aghast right about now. After all, who would admit out loud that they are rich and successful? The politically correct among us think being wealthy is something to feel guilty about, or at the very least that it is not something one should proudly announce. I suppose if I had been *born* rich that might be true. Perhaps I'd feel guilty or ashamed at possessing wealth I hadn't earned. Perhaps I'd want to hide from my wealth. But I wasn't born rich. I was born with nothing. I was born an S.O.B.—Son of a Butcher! I was born on the wrong side of the tracks, raised in a blue-collar town on the border of the Bronx. But I was also raised to become a Millionaire Republican. David Root, my blue-collar butcher father, was the single biggest influence on my life. His story changed my life and put me on the path to wealth and success. The first lesson my butcher father ever taught me was this: The Republican Party is not just the party of the rich. It's the party of anyone who *wants* to be rich! Anyone with hope. Anyone with dreams. Anyone who desires the freedom and the opportunity to achieve wealth and independence. Anyone willing to work for it.

The fact that today I am a Millionaire Republican is something of which I am very proud—and I'll shout it from the rooftops! Success should be celebrated and emulated. That's how we encourage and empower others to become wealthy and successful. I beat almost insurmountable odds. But Millionaire Republicans do that every day. We are the daring risk-takers of the business world. We thrive on making the impossible *possible.* It's been quite a journey to go from S.O.B. to self-made millionaire, CEO, author, and television celebrity. This book is the story of how I got there, and it is also an in-

struction manual that will teach you how *you* can go from wherever you are now—no matter how humble your beginnings or
hopeless your current circumstances seem—to become a Millionaire Republican yourself. I am living proof that the American
Dream is alive and well. If I can rise from the rough-and-tumble
streets of Mount Vernon, New York, to find fortune, then so can
you. If I can go from misery to millionaire, then so can you! But
to put the odds in your favor, you're going to need to learn and
live by the 18 Republican Secrets of Mega-Wealth and Unlimited
Success. That's what this book is all about—teaching you these
valuable principles and rules, and how to live by them, just as my
blue-collar butcher father taught me.

This book wasn't written for millionaires or Republicans, although I'm certain those groups will buy it and love it. It wasn't
written for business executives or small-business owners, although I'm certain they too will buy it and love it. *Millionaire Republican* was written for the rest of the world that is fighting and
getting nowhere fast, struggling to stay ahead of the bill collec-
tors, paying off the mortgage, and trying *unsuccessfully* to build
assets and wealth. It was written for minorities and immigrants
who desperately want a piece of the American Dream but have
been held back by thinking like poor Democrats. It was written
for single mothers who struggle to survive at jobs they hate
(jobs they rent, instead of *own*), all the while believing the Liberal Democrat propaganda about how "unfair" life is, how the
deck is stacked against the poor, against minorities and women;
how hopeless it is for ordinary Americans to attain wealth.

(Well, of course it is—if you listen to crap like *that!*) It was written for young adults stuck in classrooms listening to the advice and wisdom of people who are "book smart" but ignorant in the topic of "street smarts," and uneducated about achieving wealth in the real world. This book was written for everyone who still believes in the power of the American Dream, everyone who hungers to tell their boss to "shove it" and become their own boss, everyone who wants to *own* instead of rent their future. If you still have the burning desire, the fire, the hunger of a champion, but don't know how to go from here to there, *Millionaire Republican* was written for you. And if time or circumstances make it too late for you, use this book to teach your children and grandchildren the attitude and mind-set they need (as my blue-collar butcher father did for me), so the *next* generation of your family can become Millionaire Republicans.

This book is about *opportunity.* Opportunity is everywhere. You just need to change your mind-set. You need to learn the rules—the Republican Rules! You need to be hungry for wealth and success (actually, you need to be *starving*). You need to understand how to identify opportunity—or better yet, how to create it out of thin air. And then you must be prepared to take the daring risks necessary to *seize* it. You must go after it aggressively, passionately, and with abandon, then capture it and drag it home—just like a *caveman!* On more than one occasion, I've heard Liberal Democrats call rich Republicans "Neanderthals." Well, I *accept!* Achieving wealth isn't for the weak, meek, sensitive, passive, or faint of heart. You need to be a caveman. You need to be an aggressive, rugged individualist with big dreams and a willingness to take even bigger risks. Liberal Democrats wince at hearing words like this. These are *fighting* words— action, aggression, attack, seize, risk, fight, capture, courage, commitment. These words are the vocabulary of Millionaire Republicans. They strike fear in the very heart of liberaldom. As everyone knows, sensitive liberals are scared of battle, gun-shy, offended by aggression, unwilling to fight even a necessary fight. Heck, they're afraid of hurting people's *feelings!*

Liberals think I should be ashamed of my aggressive nature, my unbridled passion for wealth, my remarkable rags-to-riches story. But I am not! I have no reason to hide in the closet. I am proud of where I've come from, what I've achieved after start-ing with nothing, and who I am today. I dreamed it, I believed it, I planned it, and I worked my plan. I turned my dream into a reality against incredible odds. My dream of achieving wealth is the American Dream. The quintessential American Dream is all about financial freedom—always has been, always will be. If that's your dream too, there's no need to hide your ambition anymore. You picked up this book. You want what I've got. You want to *own* instead of rent your job, your future, your life. As that wise butcher from Brooklyn, David Root, once said, "The Republican Party is the party of anyone who *wants* to become rich."

Admit it—you want to become rich. You want it badly. We all do! I'm here to bring out the Millionaire Republican that's in all of us.

· 1 ·

Saving Kassandra

The lack of money is the root of all evil.

—MARK TWAIN

Shortly after I decided to write *Millionaire Republican,* I was sitting down in my office to answer some e-mail and begin putting pen to paper (or, more concisely, keyboard to hard drive), when my wife, Debra, stuck her head around the corner and said, "Wayne, stop what you're doing—you *have* to see this television show." Now, I rarely watch television, except for sporting events (which, as I'll explain later, is part of my work). As you'll learn throughout this book, becoming a Millionaire Republican requires tremendous amounts of risk-taking, tenacity, courage, commitment, chutzpah, discipline, and sacrifice. TV is one of the things I usually sacrifice. On most nights, I do not watch any. But this night was different.

I looked up and saw tears in Debra's eyes. "Honey, you need to see this show, it is truly amazing," she said as she headed back to the living room. In addition to being my wife, Debra is my confidante and the mother of my three beautiful young children—Dakota (thirteen years old), Hudson (five years old), and Remington Reagan (one year old). When she says I really need to see something, I *know* it's important. So I reluctantly left my laptop to play the dutiful husband. It turned out to have been a wise decision.

The show was called *Extreme Home Makeover*. This episode was about an incredible little girl named Kassandra, from Gilbert, Arizona. Kassandra had just undergone treatment for cancer. She and her family had literally been through hell. They were poor, living in a ramshackle house—with the added burden of a serious mold problem. Now, mold is a terrible thing under normal circumstances, making even healthy people sick. Can you imagine the horrible circumstances of an eight-year-old girl suffering from cancer, with a bald head from undergoing traumatic chemotherapy, having to breathe in toxic mold in her own home? And just imagine the guilt and pain her parents are going through, knowing that with every breath that precious little girl could get sicker and sicker? Can you imagine knowing your child may die, that her life hangs in the balance, and that you cannot remove that deadly mold? And why can't you remove it? Because of a lack of money.

They say timing is everything in life. Well, in this case it was a matter of life and death. This tragic story suddenly turned wonderful when the cavalry (courtesy of ABC) rode to the rescue. The *Extreme Home Makeover* design team charged onto the scene to rescue the family and hand Kassandra the life of her dreams. This is where the story gets really good. What, exactly, did Kassandra ask ABC for? Not a fancy new home for her family. No, she asked only for an extreme makeover of the children's ward of the University Medical Center in Tucson, where she had just spent so many painful and sad days. Even while facing death, this precious little angel thought only of the happiness of *others.* Her dream was not for herself, it was to enrich the lives of the *other* children in that cancer ward. We all know that macho guys don't cry. Well, on this night, tears flowed in the Root household.

I am happy to report that ABC and the *Extreme Home Makeover* team rose to the occasion by making this the most special and expensive home makeover ever. First, they sent the design team to redo that children's ward. Then, while Kassandra and her family were in Tucson overseeing the hospital makeover, ABC set out to present them with the surprise of a lifetime! In one week, they bulldozed Kassandra's home and built her a new one! And not just any new home—they erected a spectacular 5,400-square-foot state-of-the-art *mansion,* filled with the latest and greatest of everything—from plasma screens to Sub-Zero freezers. After Kassandra and her family had seen their incredible new home, they were presented with an even bigger surprise. Not only were they given this incredible new mansion free of charge, the construction company paid off the mortgage on their old home! My God, if you don't cry over this story you're already dead, so stop reading! It was the most heart-wrenching and heart-warming show I've ever watched.

As the show ended, I was so happy for Kassandra that my heart almost burst.

What did it take to change the lives of Kassandra and this family that had suffered so much? *It took a whole lot of wealth!* It took the amazing generosity of ABC, Sears, a major construction company, and the *Extreme Home Makeover* design team. All things considered (building a new mansion in a week, filling it with expensive furnishings, ripping up the mortgage, filming a TV production around the whole event), my educated guess is that "Saving Kassandra" cost a few million dollars! That's the cost to take a struggling, hardworking, lower-middle-class family suffering from a health crisis and give them a dream life overnight. That's the cost of turning Kassandra and her family into instant Millionaire Republicans—just a few million dollars here and a few million dollars there. But hey, it's only money.

My point in telling this story? To prove to you that wealth is a *blessing.* Wealth is amazing, magical, wondrous, life-enhancing, life-affirming, and life-changing. I believe we were all meant to be wealthy. Unfortunately, it just doesn't happen for most of us. Or, to put it more bluntly, most of us just don't know *how* to become wealthy. Wouldn't it be great if every American could live the life of a millionaire? Wouldn't it be great if we could magically transform all the Kassandras into Cinderellas? Wouldn't it be great if all of us had the money to build our dream house, free of a mortgage, and provide our kids with a healthy, pure, cancer-free environment? Maybe our kids wouldn't get sick in the first place. But if they did, we wouldn't have to worry about medical bills, deductibles, or losing our health insurance.

But that's not the way it is for most of us. Kassandra isn't an isolated incident. I watch *Extreme Home Makeover* every week now. I love the show (probably because I'm a positive thinker and love the happy endings). But every week features a new Kassandra. Whether eight years old, or eighteen, or thirty-eight, or seventy-eight, every week *Extreme Home Makeover* brings us a new tragedy—starting with helpless, hopeless, aimless families suffering a living hell. They are all nice people. None of them deserve the pain and poverty they're living in. But unfortunately, bad things (bad *financial* things) happen to good people all the time—especially if they've never learned the rules of wealth, never learned to think like a Millionaire Republican. The people featured each week on *Extreme Home Makeover* are so far in a hole that it takes a miracle to save them. Isn't it pathetic and a shame that only ABC and millions of dollars can provide that miracle?

I wrote *Millionaire Republican* because it's a crime that people have to live this way and that so many smart, capable, loving, salt-of-the-earth families live in utter hopelessness and helplessness waiting for a miracle, or Lotto, or Big Brother, or ABC to save them. For one family each week, the prayers are answered. But millions of others never get that miracle. Their lives are an endless living hell. Yet it doesn't have to be that way. I firmly believe that everyone in this great country has the potential to provide dream lives for their own families—just as

ABC and the *Extreme Home Makeover* team provided for Kassandra and her family. My favorite saying is "Everything is easy if you know what to do." My goals are to teach you what to do, say, think, and how to act, to unravel the great mysteries about wealth; to give anyone and everyone the attitude, mind-set, and tools to achieve the American Dream, to create *owners* instead of renters, and ultimately to save millions of Kassandras!

Unfortunately, in today's America that is no easy task. A significant portion of the population has given up on ever achieving the American Dream. Ironically, to many Americans the idea of mega-wealth and unlimited success is *foreign*. They have come to accept a life of surviving, instead of *thriving*. They have been taught to think small, to feel inferior, to accept limitations, and to dumb down expectations.

Who is responsible for destroying hope, instilling fear, encouraging negativity and mediocrity? Who has killed the American Dream? I blame one group for all this damage: *Liberal Democrats*. It's no mistake or coincidence that Kassandra is helpless. Liberal Democratic thinking put her (and millions like her) in this predicament. How? By not even allowing a discussion about wealth in our educational system in the first place. By choosing to keep our children ignorant about the topic of wealth, so that many young Americans aren't even aware that wealth is an option. According to those running our education system, we are much better off teaching our Kassandras to play it safe—to find a "safe job" and spend the rest of their lives collecting a "safe" (but mediocre) paycheck. They teach our kids the exact wrong strategy—to rent instead of own. The result is that most Americans live like Kassandra and her family—lives of despair and disappointment, just barely surviving, always one paycheck away from disaster, working in jobs they hate, for bosses they despise, biding their time for retirement and a miserable dependency on a measly Social Security check. Forever renting instead of owning—at the mercy of fate, and dependent on Big Brother.

That's what safety creates: a lifetime of renting. Safety leads to a dependence on the "safety net." Liberal Democrats are the reason so many Americans are ignorant, fearful, and uncomfortable about wealth. They are the reason that so many Americans are hopeless, helpless, aimless, and clueless. It is because of liberal thinking that there are so many Kassandras. And why do Liberal Democrats want to keep us ignorant, hopeless, jealous, and fearful about wealth? So we'll desperately *need* them! So we'll keep them in power. So we'll vote Democrat and remain dependent on the Liberal Democrat entitlement machine. So the leaders of the Democratic Party can retain power and perks—keeping control over jobs, federal entitlement programs, pork-barrel spending, and the government bureaucracy. I call this evil business "Poverty Inc."

Are these the kinds of lessons you want your kids being taught? Do you want you and your family to rent for the rest of your lives? Or do you want to own a piece of the American Dream? Do you want to live a life of dependence, fear, and hopelessness? Of course not! The proof is that you've picked up this book. You desire a different kind of education, from a different kind of role model—the *right* kind! You've chosen to escape the liberal propaganda machine that condemns Kassandra and millions like her to a lifetime of poverty and mediocrity, to a lifetime of renting—their homes, jobs, retirements, and lives. Kassandra got lucky. ABC came to her rescue. But most of us will not be that lucky. Most of us will never win the lottery or get a TV network to spend several million dollars on us. Yet there are *millions* of Kassandras in America and *billions* in the world. ABC can't ride in like the cavalry, carrying a Brinks truck, for everyone. The rest of us had better learn how to fend for ourselves! The rest of us need to learn the attitude, mindset, tools, and skills required to succeed, to thrive, to own—to become Millionaire Republicans. I'm going to teach you something in this book that scares the hell out of Liberal Democrats and government bureaucrats—*how to own and control your own life!*

To go from where you are today to Millionaire Republican status you must plan your success step by step. Then you must work your plan. I'll teach you how to do that later in this book. But first, you must believe that the American Dream is real and alive. You must believe, beyond a shadow of a doubt, that your own personal dream is possible. You must believe that wealth is a good thing, an empowering thing. You must believe that wealth is a worthy and achievable goal. You must believe, deep down, that you *deserve* success and wealth. You must understand that it is a *lack* of money that ruins lives, that causes despair, that forces so many people to settle. It is a *lack* of money that results in lives filled with pain and disappointment. It is the *lack* of money that is the root of all evil. Then you must go after your dream by applying the 18 Republican Secrets of Mega-Wealth and Unlimited Success. The way to create a better life for all the Kassandras of this world is to educate more people about wealth and success. Teaching more Americans how to own instead of rent their homes, jobs, retirement, and lives is the answer. *More wealth is the answer.* Not more taxes. Not more government regulations. Not more government programs. Not more dependence on Big Brother.

It's time for Lesson One, and it starts with a confession. The truth is that deep down *everyone* wants to be wealthy. C'mon, admit it. You'd love to live the life of a Millionaire Republican. *Confess.* You really do want to live in a mansion, drive exotic cars, wear expensive designer clothes, eat at glamorous restaurants, and travel the world in style. You really do want to give a better life to your children. It's nothing to be ashamed of. It's *not* greedy. On the contrary, it is a goal worthy of your pursuit *every* minute of every day. Everyone, regardless of what they admit out loud, wants to live the life of a millionaire. Even poor Democrats secretly wish they could live the lives of Millionaire Republicans! If they didn't, no one would play Lotto. No one would watch *Extreme Home Makeover,* or *Who Wants to Be a Millionaire,* or *The Apprentice,* or *American Idol,* or *Survivor.* The biggest hits on television all revolve around becoming instantly wealthy and living the dream life—the life of a millionaire. The problem is that these shows are the equivalent of eating fast food. They're bad for you. They make you fat, lazy, and unrealistic. Except for a few lucky lottery winners (and a few Hollywood stars), wealth is *never* instant. "Overnight success" almost always requires years of hard work and sacrifice. And it almost never has anything to do with luck. Most millionaires will tell you that the harder they worked, the luckier they got! But most of all, achieving wealth requires knowledge. No, not the kind of book smarts you learn at school. You've simply got to understand how the game is played. You must learn the *right* rules— the Republican Rules. You must understand the mechanics of wealth—how and why some get wealthy, and why most do not. Self-made millionaires are not born. They earn every penny of it.

There's only one way out for most of us. Repeat after me: If it is to be, it is up to me. *You* are the answer. But first you'll have to reprogram the negative, hopeless, helpless liberal crap out of your subconscious. You'll need to learn to play by a new set of rules: The 18 Republican Secrets of Mega-Wealth and Unlimited Success. You have the potential—we all do. You've come to the right class. You're now a student in the *Investor Class.* You're among friends, so you don't have to keep your secret desire of becoming a Millionaire Republican a secret anymore. That dream of yours is no longer a pipe dream. Wealth is no longer a dirty word. To crave millions of dollars is not a sin. To want to give that dream life to your kids is not a sin. To want to be your own boss and build your own business is not a sin. To want to retire in style is not a sin. Confess, my friends. You'll feel much better! We all want to be Kassandra after ABC turned her into Cinderella! We all want to live the American Dream. We all want to be Millionaire Republicans (whether you vote Republican or not—although once you finish this book, I think you'll agree that you're a damn fool if you don't). This book is filled with practical steps to achieve that dream and empower you to become your own self-made Millionaire Republican. It took a miracle and millions of dollars provided by ABC to change Kassandra's life. But Millionaire Republicans don't depend on miracles from others. We create and build our own miracles! Join me on the journey of a lifetime.

It's time for your Extreme Republican Makeover!

· 2 ·

The Divided States of America

MILLIONAIRE REPUBLICANS OWN, DEMOCRATS RENT

Lincoln was not great because he was born in a log cabin,

but because he got out of it.

—JAMES TRUSLOW ADAMS

This entire book comes down to one thing: ownership. Own, don't rent. Owners have power and control. Renters are powerless, helpless, and rudderless. They live their lives in fear and desperation. They require government to protect and rescue them. Renters have no control. Everything in their lives comes down to Big Brother: big corporations, big government, big entitlement programs, the landlord, the union leader, the local Democratic Party boss. Renters are followers, not leaders. They do whatever the boss orders them to do. Remember what my dad, the poor Brooklyn butcher, said about the Republican Party? That it's the party of anyone who *wants* to be rich. It's the party of freedom. Being rich goes hand in hand with freedom and *ownership*. You can't get rich until you own your own life, own your future, until you have the freedom to make your own decisions. If you have to listen to the orders of others, or depend on a weekly paycheck from others, you will never be rich. It's that simple. Own, don't rent. My father, David Root, taught me that philosophy almost forty years ago. He had no idea how right he was!

You know what you call someone who wants to be rich? A member of the "Investor Class." A member of the Investor Class is not necessarily rich yet, but he or she *owns*—or strives to own—a piece of the pie, a piece of the American Dream: a home, investment property, stocks, a small business, or even their own retirement account (think privatization of Social Security). They yearn to own instead of rent. They are card-carrying members of the new "Ownership Society." Kassandra's family owned nothing. They were typical Democrats, victims, dependent on the generosity of government or of strangers like ABC. What a sad way to live life. When you own, you don't need to feel helpless or hopeless. When you own, you don't need to depend on help from anyone. When you own, you are the captain of your own ship. Owning gives you *power*.

I believe that ownership is the most important issue for the future of American politics. A recent poll by Zogby International puts it all in perspective. Zogby found that few questions are more accurate for identifying how an American will vote than asking him or her if they are a member of the Investor Class. It's that simple. The dramatic results of this Zogby poll were reported in the *Wall Street Journal* shortly after the 2004 election. Americans who considered themselves members of the Investor Class voted 61 to 39 percent in favor of George W. Bush (a landslide 22-point victory for the GOP). Those who didn't consider themselves members of the Investor Class voted 57 to 42 percent in favor of John Kerry (a landslide 15-point victory for the Democrats). That's a 37 percent differential in how investors (or at least those who would like to see themselves as investors) voted versus noninvestors. So in fact, success-oriented Americans vote predominantly Republican. People with ambition, drive, vision, courage, confidence, and commitment are the driving force of Republican politics! People who are owners and investors, or who *want* to be owners or investors, or *see* themselves as owners or investors, tend to think like, vote for, and support the Republican Party. These success-oriented Americans are the very definition of Millionaire Republicans.

The members of this Investor Class are creating a new American Revolution—at least a political one. I call it the Red Storm! Americans who invest and own (or want to) are migrating in record numbers to red states, buying homes, buying stocks, and starting businesses in record numbers (primarily in red states). And as their ranks grow, the GOP will dominate as never before. They are the reason why this professional prognosticator sees historic political realignment in favor of the Republican Party, the likes of which has not been seen since FDR and the Democratic Party started a half century of political dominance in 1932. (I'll present more details on this historic Red Storm in a later chapter). But what is happening is pretty simple: More Americans than ever are owning homes, owning stocks, starting and owning businesses. And people who own anything tend to vote Republican. That is leading to a divided country—two very different Americas. It's red states versus blue states, rich versus poor, hope versus hopeless, haves versus have-nots, opportunity versus desperation, dependence versus independence—but most of all, it's own versus rent. Americans with more education, smarts, creativity, ambition, energy, moxie, and *money* are moving in droves out of blue (Democratic) states and into red (Republican) states. I call it "The Divided States of America."

This population shift and political realignment is creating a power paradigm—blue states are being sucked dry by a historic "brain drain." As young, bright, educated, ambitious Americans with vibrant careers, big dreams, and lots of money (because they own homes, stocks, businesses) leave the blue states, these old aging Democratic dinosaurs (states like New York, New Jersey, Connecticut, Pennsylvania, California, Illinois, and Massachusetts) are left with populations that desperately depend on Big Brother for *everything*. The people left in these blue decaying regions need more services, more medical care (the old left behind are aging, the young are reckless and suffer from drug and alcohol abuse), more entitlements, more police (because of higher crime rates), and more jobs (government has to create jobs, because these are not people who are capable of creating their own). Opportunities, jobs, money, and hope are all in short supply in blue, Democrat-dominated states, whereas red states are filled with young, vibrant Millionaire Republicans. That in turn creates a vicious cycle. Red states gain electoral votes and congressional seats—meaning more political power and more access to wealth and opportunity. Blue states are left with crumbs—a smaller piece of the pie that must be shared with ever higher numbers of needy people (incapable of creating ownership for themselves). You have to choose. Which group do you want to join? Are you interested in capitalizing on this historic power shift? Do you want to own or rent? Do you know what specifically to own or invest in, in this new Red Storm? Read on—*Millionaire Republican* was written for you!

Do you know what's so great about being a Republican in the midst of this red revolution? The GOP is the party of positive thinkers and positive goals. Our goals are to uplift, encourage, and empower this new wave of big thinkers. We want and *need* to create more owners and more successful Americans. We need to create more stockholders and home owners and business owners. We need to create more millionaires. We want you to own a piece of the American Dream, but not because Republicans are so selfless or benevolent or charitable or wonderful. Let me be honest and blunt: We're being selfish. We want you to become successful because the facts prove that once you own instead of rent, you'll start to think and vote like a Republican! So our goals are aligned with yours. Our goal is to encourage success, to empower all Americans to dream big, think big, achieve big. But it doesn't matter what our reasons are—selfish or not. In the end, we are on your side. That's all you need to know.

But the more important point to consider is the sad plight of Democrats. To win elections, they need to keep their voters fearful and desperate. They need their voters to think small. They need their voters to rent instead of own—even though ownership is the American Dream. In order to win elections, Democrats depend on keeping their voters ignorant, hopeless, helpless, and clueless! They cannot allow their voters to even *think* of living the American Dream. They cannot allow their voters to even *think* of investing in stocks, or owning a home, or starting a small business, because anyone who succeeds in owning a piece of the American Dream will vote predominantly Republican. That means the best interests of Democrat politicians and strategists are in direct opposition to your goals! Their goal is to keep you poor and helpless. Can you imagine? The proven ways to get rich in America are through the ownership of stocks, real estate, and your own business, i.e., becoming a member of the Investor Class described by Zogby. But Liberal Democrats have a vested interest in never allowing you to own *anything*. Instead of pushing and pulling and empowering their voters to think positive and dream big and risk big and attain wealth—which is the GOP game plan—Democrats preach fear and negativity and discourage success.

Democrats want you to rent forever. They want you stuck in a dead-end job (i.e., renting your career), renting your apartment, and renting your future (desperately depending on government entitlements and measly Social Security checks in your golden years). They don't want to privatize Social Security, because then you'd own your own retirement plan. It would be yours to take wherever you go and to leave to your kids. But as the Zogby poll proves, any form of ownership results in people voting Republican. Democrats couldn't allow that, now could they? Older Americans might abandon the Democratic Party in droves if they felt that they were part of the Investor Class. So desperate Democrats and government bureaucrats must go on the attack against policies like the privatization of Social Security—no matter how good it is for seniors, no matter if it can save Social Security from bankruptcy, no matter if liberal government bureaucrats already invest their pension plans in stocks. Liberal Democrats desperately *need* you to stay ignorant about stocks, real estate, and business ownership. Because the less you own, the more fearful you feel. The more *left* out (excuse the pun), angry, and resentful you feel, the farther away you feel from being an owner, the higher the odds you'll vote Democrat. How sad. How *evil*.

No wonder the Republican Party will dominate the next century. Which team would you rather play on? The choice is so obvious. Millions of Americans are voting with their hands (pulling the Republican lever), with their feet (moving to red states), and with their wallets (by buying homes, stocks, and small businesses in record numbers). Given a clear choice, the majority of Americans always choose opportunity and wealth.

They choose to own instead of rent. They choose economic freedom and independence over dependence on big government and massive entitlement programs. They choose optimism and opportunity over pessimism, bitterness, jealousy, and resentment. They choose hope over hopelessness. The fact is, as Zogby showed, a majority of Americans yearn to become members of the Investor Class. The future of America and the future success of the Republican Party is all about creating more owners instead of renters. It is about creating more Millionaire Republicans. More rich Republican dads (and kids) instead of poor, helpless, hopeless Democrat dads (and their children—like Kassandra). More dads able to give their children a better life instead of watching hopelessly as their children live (or die) in pain and poverty.

Republicans understand that we must lift others up and give everyone hope and opportunity. Whereas the Democratic philosophy is to tear down the rich and encourage the renters of the world to hate or resent the owners. Their aim is to redistribute the wealth. *It doesn't work.* You can't get rich by tearing others down. You can't get rich by taking from others (Robin Hood was a fairy tale). No, Republicans are not saints or selfless. We want you to vote Republican. But we know the best way to get you to do that is to help you grow rich! Isn't that pretty cool? Our goals are aligned. The richer, more successful, and independent you get, the more likely we'll be to win you over to our side. Thank God that we've got the winning message! With a message like that, with goals like that, the GOP will dominate American politics for the next half-century and beyond!

This book is dedicated to showing you how to thrive (instead of survive), how to own (instead of rent), in this new red world. What's amazing is that my dad, David Root, the poor butcher from Brooklyn, understood that thinking forty years ago. I loved my dad very much. I think about him every single day. He was a remarkable man. He gave up his dreams so I could live mine. He is my hero. He is literally the father of the Millionaire Republican philosophy. Can you imagine? Forty years ago a poor butcher from Brooklyn developed the philosophy that today creates owners and millionaires. Only in America! I think it's time you met David Root.

· 3 ·

My Father's Story

THE REPUBLICAN BUTCHER
FROM BROOKLYN

The Republican Party is not just the party of the rich.
It's the party of anyone who wants to be rich.

—DAVID ROOT

I have defined my life by being an S.O.B.—Son of a Butcher. I'll always be the S.O.B. from Mount Vernon, New York. And I'll always be my father's son. My father, David Root, was born into a life of abject poverty, one of seven children born to a single mother in the crime-ridden Brownsville section of Brooklyn, New York. His father, my grandfather Louis Root, died in the "poor ward" of a Brooklyn hospital. By the time I was born, my parents, David and Stella, had moved to Mount Vernon, on the Bronx border. My maternal grandfather owned a butcher shop nearby. My father worked for my grandfather and went to that butcher shop every day of his working life. His influence on me was powerful. This book would never have been written if it weren't for him. His story, and his choices in life, changed my life and made me a self-made success. This is my father's story.

To tell his story, I need to begin at the end. At the age of sixty-seven, my father was lying on his deathbed, dying of cancer with me, his only son, by his side. He had lived his life like most men of his generation: as an honest, hardworking family man, a devoted husband and father.

But he was also a sad man who knew that along the way he had given up on his dreams and settled for a life of mediocrity. When I was born, he was thirty-five years old and already a broken man. I never once heard him complain, but I also never heard him talk about his dreams or goals. I had just assumed he'd never had any.

Now, as the sun was setting outside the tightly closed blinds of my father's hospital-room window, me sitting beside his bed holding his hand, he began to speak slowly. "Wayne, every day of my life I hated working at that butcher shop. I just went to work every day, earning a living and supporting my family."

I remembered how he arrived home every night physically exhausted, but I'd never realized before that he was also emotionally drained. By the time he reached his deathbed, he had worked for over forty years in a dead-end, blue-collar job that he despised. He justified this lifetime of long hours for mediocre pay as a necessary sacrifice for his family. Ironically, he rarely ever saw that family. In those days, a butcher left for work at 3:30 a.m. (to go to the freezing-cold meat market and pick out the day's fresh meat) and didn't return until 7 p.m., six days a week.

Back pains plagued him most of his adult life. He literally spent his life breaking his back for a family he never saw.

As I listened and watched him dying, I saw tears come to his eyes. Only once, as a child, had I seen my father cry. It had been at a family gathering twenty-five years earlier, and he had been surrounded by his family. I had blocked this memory out for a quarter of a century. Sitting at my dying father's bedside, memories of that day came flooding back. Seven brothers and sisters, their spouses, and his mother (my grandmother Anna) were gathered around my father at the dining room table. My cousins and I had just come down the stairs, headed outside to play. He was sobbing uncontrollably. I watched for only a few seconds, then, scared, I quickly turned and ran outside. For twenty-five years I had supressed this memory. Now it felt as if it had happened yesterday. Dad was dying, and for the first time in my life he was talking to me about his feelings and his life. It was clear there were things he wanted me to know, things he felt it was important for a father to share with his son.

My father laid his hand on my arm, looked me straight in the eye, and spoke. "I hated every day of my life working as a butcher. I felt demeaned and humiliated, beneath the customers I served." He continued, "But it fed the family. It fed you, your mother, and your sister. It kept a roof over your heads. It paid your way through college. And it gave you the opportunity to pursue your dreams." He closed his eyes and rested.

More memories flooded my mind. I remembered my father, especially when I was very young, talking nonstop about all of the wonderful places that existed in the world, saying that someday he was going to explore them all. It was then that I realized he had never gone *anywhere*. And at that moment, I realized he felt he had no choice. He had felt trapped—he had had a family to feed. So he had done the only thing he believed he could do. He kept trudging to that damned butcher shop for forty years.

A few minutes later he reopened his eyes, seeming stronger, and smiled at me. I asked him if he remembered the day twenty-five years before, in our dining room, when I'd seen him crying, surrounded by his family. "You remember that day?" he asked.

"Yes," I replied. "It was the only time I ever saw you cry."

My father fell silent for a moment, and then he spoke. "I've tried to be a good father. I may have been stuck in a life I hated, my options may have been limited, but I did everything I could to be sure that you could be anything or anyone you chose. I wanted to be sure that your options were unlimited. On that day when you saw me cry, I had confided in my family that I was struggling with the idea of quitting my job and leaving your mother."

He told me it was a crossroad in his life and that the entire family had talked him out of it. They had convinced him that he couldn't leave, that he couldn't abandon his wife, his daughter, and his only son. No, he had agreed, that was something he simply couldn't do. He told me that after that emotional breakdown in front of his family, he had buried his dreams for the very last time. "I never allowed myself to think about them again," he said. "I went back to the job I hated for twenty-five more years. On that day twenty-five years ago, I gave up all my dreams."

I sat stunned. It is said that when a man's dreams die, the man dies too. I had no doubt that a major part of my father died that day twenty-five years before. He had given up any chance at passion, at happiness, at truly living, at *thriving* instead of merely surviving. He had settled for an *existence* instead of a life.

Just then the nurse came in with Dad's evening medications. He asked her to open the blinds so he could watch the last of the sunset. As she left the room, I scooted my chair back to my father's beside. I was eager to hear more. I asked him about the travel stories he had told us. "I've never seen you travel anywhere. Why?" I asked. His eyes got bright, and he broke into a smile and explained that long before I was born, he had been a traveler, an explorer, a courageous fighter. Suddenly I learned about a man I had never known. As a teenager during World War II, my father had left Brooklyn to attend Navy navigator school at Texas A&M. Then he'd traveled halfway around the world to fight the Japanese in the South Pacific. He had won numerous distinguished-service awards at the battles of Saipan and Okinawa. Still in the Navy after the war, he had traveled to Europe and Japan. Then he'd found paradise—Hawaii. He'd spent time at Pearl Harbor before heading back to America. He loved Hawaii and vowed he'd live there

someday. After the war, he became one of the youngest naviga-
tors in the air for TWA. At the age of twenty-three, he was the
navigator on transatlantic flights from New York to London
and Hamburg, Germany, while most of his friends had never
even left Brooklyn.

My dad flying in a cockpit across the Atlantic? I thought. *Impossible!*
The father I knew had always been afraid to leave the butcher
store, afraid to leave Mount Vernon, New York. He was scared
about virtually everything I did. He wouldn't even allow me to
go away to college—he demanded I go to college nearby and
live at home. The father I knew was afraid of his own shadow.

He spoke again. "I used to drive a red convertible. I was quite
the dashing ladies' man." He told me stories of being a successful gambler. He'd played craps on the streets of Brooklyn, then
poker in the Navy and after the war. He'd used his winnings to
buy the convertible. This was *not* the man that I had known as
my father. A convertible sports car? He'd been driving nothing
but four-door Oldsmobiles since I'd been born. A gambler? To
the best of my knowledge, he hadn't made a bet in the thirty
years I'd been alive. I'd never seen him take any risk! *This definitely
isn't the father I know,* I thought to myself.

My father grew quiet and the story of the swashbuckling
navigator abruptly ended. But he wasn't done. Dad took a deep
breath and told me about meeting my mother. He said he'd
quickly fallen in love and asked her to marry him. She'd said
yes, but only with the very clear understanding that he settle
down for the sake of marriage and family. She did not want to

be married to an airline navigator. She was afraid of the risk of losing him to a plane crash. And she was deathly afraid of the loneliness, with him away so often. She wanted a husband who was home every night. Her father, the owner of a butcher store, asked my father to work for him. Dad loved my mother and quickly accepted.

"I now realize," he said, "that the day I accepted that job was the day I lost my life. My dreams all died that day. I settled." He made it clear that although his body lay dying here with me today, his actual death had started on that day forty years earlier. I just sat, stunned at what I was hearing.

For the first time in my life I realized what my father had sacrificed for me—*everything*. He had not been the passionless man I thought him to be. He had had dreams and goals. He had had ambition and determination. He had been a far different person before "life got in the way." Then I suddenly realized that everyone starts out this way—full of energy, confidence, dreams, and life. And somewhere along the way most of us lose that energy, give up on our dreams, give in to the fears, and settle.

By far the most important thing I learned sitting beside my dying father was how much I am like him. I had always thought that I had been dropped down the wrong chimney. But that night, I realized that I was actually a chip off the old block. The tears continued to flow as we both realized that my father had had his life choked out of him before I was even born. He had been taught that family was more important than dreams or self. That once a man was married with children, dreams are out. Risks are unacceptable. He was taught to play it safe for the sake of his children.

And then, of course, there was my mother. My mother was afraid of life. She was afraid to dream. To her, dreaming meant risking, and risking meant dying. She stopped my father from flying because the dangers of a plane crashing made flying an unacceptable risk. She stopped my father from swimming in the ocean (even though he had been a fearless ocean swimmer in the Navy) because the dangers of drowning rendered swimming an unacceptable risk. She stopped him from working for TWA because the dangers of him having independence, and perhaps leaving her, were a risk she could never accept.

Now before you think that I blame my mother for my father's life (or lack of it), let me set the record straight: My father's life was his own. The decisions he made were his own. My mother had a different set of goals. Her goals were to be home with her family and raise her children in a comfortable, risk-free environment. Stella accomplished her goals, David did not. I loved them both. But until that moment, I just never realized how different their goals were. And how that difference changed my father's life.

Then Dad reached over and grabbed my arm. He told me of his one last hope during all those dreadful years. He dreamed of taking an around-the-world trip before he died. He told me that he had secretly decided a few years back that he would take this world trip as a retirement gift to himself. He'd decided that he would give my mother an ultimatum: join him or he'd go alone. But before he ever retired, before he could live this last dream, he found out that he had terminal cancer. He was going to die. He would never take his trip. He would never see Hawaii again. He would never see the life I had built in California. He would never leave the hospital bed he was in. And he didn't. He died a few days later.

My father's story is a sad story. But it is also a hopeful story because it changed my life. It inspired me to go for my dreams with gusto, passion, and abandon, and to let no rock stand unturned. As a result of my father losing his dreams, I vowed to live mine. Sitting in that hospital room, I recognized that life is too short to settle for mediocrity. After listening to my dad's story, I made the commitment to myself that I'd rather die trying to achieve my dreams than "settle." I've never settled again—not for a moment, not over anything, big or small.

This book is the story of the only son of David Root, a poor butcher from the streets of Brownsville, Brooklyn. It is the story of the grandson of Louis Root, who died in the poor ward of a Brooklyn hospital. It is the story of the experiences of a son who came to understand, in a hospital room with his dying father, the secrets of success. It is the story of an S.O.B. turned self-made Millionaire Republican.

My father's life of mediocrity had a silver lining—at least for me. His poor choices inspired me to think positive, think big, dream big, and risk big. But before that night, I never understood the "why" of my father's existence. Why had he settled?

Why had he given up his dreams? In his last hours, those questions were finally answered. I finally understood why he had no passion, no dreams, and no zest for living: fear. Fear had ruled his life. Like so many others, my father settled because of a fear of failure, a fear of risk, a fear of inadequacy, a fear of being unable to survive without help from Big Brother (from government, from the boss, or in this case from the father-in-law). Fear kills more dreams and more lives than cancer ever could. A life lived in fear is a wasted life. A waste of potential. A waste of passion. A waste of the precious gift of life, of free will, bestowed upon us by God. Fear causes people to just *survive* day to day. My dad survived for all those years as a butcher, but the price he paid was way too high. He paid with his life. Cancer was just the final curtain—the play had closed at "intermission" many years before. Subconsciously, I had seen it happen, and deep down, at an early age, I had vowed that I would never let my father's fate become mine. I determined to never settle. I would never accept a life of mediocrity or "safety." I would never work for others. I would be my own man. I would make my own decisions. No boss would rule me. No fears would intimidate me. No critics could make me doubt myself. I would never be dependent on anyone—not a boss, wife, big corporation, union, father-in-law, or government. I would be free, independent, and in control of my own life.

I recognized at a young age that you pay the ultimate price for security or "help." It doesn't matter if it's your daddy, your boss, or the government. After listening to my father, in those last flickering hours of his life, I learned the defining lesson of my own life: that once you accept the security—the "safety net"—you also automatically accept *limits.* You accept compromise. You give up your dreams. You've settled. That's too big a price to pay.

I learned that lesson well: I've always dreamt big dreams, and was always willing to pay a heck of a price to make them happen. I always seemed to understand (although I never quite knew why) that if I was to make my dreams come true, I had to be a daring risk-taker. I had to throw caution and fear to the wind. I knew that to dream big and risk big meant there would be no "safe jobs," guaranteed paychecks, bosses, or butcher stores for me. I knew that the minute I settled for security, I was giving away my dreams. I understood all of that subconsciously. Now, for the first time, I understood why—because I had grown up watching and feeling my father's pain.

Quite frankly, you may be shocked to hear what I'm about to tell you: I believe security and safety are your *enemies.* They will tame you. They will take the passion, creativity, enthusiasm, and ambition out of your life. Security isn't good for any young person. It's deadly poison! It's the ultimate dream killer. And, it's sold by those well-intentioned, well-meaning people called liberals, government bureaucrats, unions, and big corporations (with their job security and "safe, steady, guaranteed paychecks"). They all want you to *settle.* They need you to need them. They need you to lower your expectations to surviving, instead of thriving. They need you to live in fear. They need you to believe you are inadequate. They desperately need you to rely on them for your paycheck and your personal identity. And do you know what happens when you do? *They own you!* They own you just like a heroin addict is owned by the drugs and the drug dealer. Your mind, your dreams, your life are all now under "their" control. You are dependent.

To succeed, to truly live the American Dream, to *thrive* and not just survive, you must throw all those fears, insecurities, and doubts out the window. You must muster all the courage, aggressiveness, tenacity, and daring risk-taking that is in you— all the chutzpah you have! And then you must *take action.* You must learn to go on the offensive, to attack aggressively and with passion. These, in a nutshell, are the Republican secrets of mega-wealth and success. Ironically, they were taught to me by my father, the blue-collar butcher. He literally gave up his life so that I would not make those same mistakes, so that I would not let fear dominate my life like it had his. So that I could become a Millionaire Republican.

Pretty simple stuff. Yet how many of us actually understand these secrets? The American Dream, I'm sorry to say, is over the minute you let fear creep into your mind and you accept the three deadly S's: safety, security, and settling. It's just as true for you as it was for my father. You'll never have that Mercedes or Hummer if you accept the safety and security of a "safe" paycheck. You'll never have that mansion or the freedom that wealth brings if you accept the safety and security of government help. You'll never become a Millionaire Republican if you aim to survive instead of thrive. If you let fear rule your life, it will snuff out your dreams!

Because I subconsciously understood my father's mistakes long ago, I had decided that my life would be nothing like his. I'd embrace risk. If I was going to lose at business or life, at least I'd go down swinging! I'd not only swing, I'd swing for the *fences*. And that's how I've lived my life. The result is that I've failed often but also tasted phenomenal levels of success. All that risk-taking, swinging for the fences, and failing is what turned this S.O.B. into a Millionaire Republican. I wrote this book to educate, empower, and inspire all of you to do the same.

So many of us are literally petrified by change, by risk, by the prospect of failure, that we'd rather do nothing than risk the pain of defeat. We'd rather live in mediocrity and misery than take a chance on our dreams. And it is all because of that dreaded F word: fear. We sell ourselves short and give up our dreams in order to merely survive. On the one side is the life of our dreams, and on the other side is a fear so strong it chokes the very life out of us. We settle and choose the fear. We'd rather depend on the security blanket of government, or a boss (with that "safe" job and guaranteed paycheck) than face the unknown (even if the unknown is filled with unlimited potential and the life of our dreams). The Liberal Machine that I call Poverty Inc. convinces the weakest among us that anything is better than the fear of going it alone without a safety net. So we give up our dreams. We give up our freedom out of a fear of inadequacy. We willingly embrace lowered expectations and mediocrity. It's sad what fear does to so many of us.

But my lesson at my dying father's bedside wasn't over just yet. As we continued to talk well into the night, I learned more about the power of fear. My father confided that he, at that very moment, was fearful for me and the life I had chosen. "Why?" I asked. His answer was telling. "Wayne, you're such a dreamer. Such a fearless entrepreneur. You've taken such huge risks in the business world. You've been disappointed so many times. You've had your heart broken and your head handed to you, over and over. You've always had such big plans—and they always seem to come crashing down. I'm so scared for your future. What's going to happen to you after I'm gone? You can't keep chasing these big dreams! You can't keep risking. You're headed for a life of pain and disappointment."

Here he was, on his deathbed, his life ending in fear, pain, and disappointment because he had never been a risk-taker, never been a dreamer, never swung for the fences (at least not since the day he got married). He had settled, and the results were devastating. Yet even on this day, he still didn't get it. He still hadn't learned his lesson, even on his deathbed. That really painted a clear picture for me. For the first time I understood the incredible power of fear. It is crippling.

At that moment, when he was so fearful for my future, let me explain what my life was like. I was a young man already living the American Dream. Things couldn't get much better for a thirty-year-old S.O.B. from the wrong side of the tracks. I was a national TV host and sports prognosticator, living on the beach in Malibu, California. I had just bought a home formerly owned by Woody Harrelson of *Cheers* fame. My neighbors were TV and movie stars. I was passionately in love with the woman of my dreams—literally a dream girl, my wife, Debra, was a former Miss Oklahoma, a model, an actress, and an accomplished singer who spoke five languages. At that moment by my father's bedside, I had my dream job, dream girl, dream home on the beach, and my first child was on the way. I was living on cloud nine! My father knew all this, yet he still feared for me. *Can you even imagine the hold fear must have had on his life?*

At that moment, the pieces of my father's puzzle came together. I finally understood why a man so talented, so bright, so loving to his family, had settled for a life of mediocrity and a job he despised. It was a fear of risk and failure so powerful that it *paralyzed* him. He was so afraid of failing that he never took a risk. He was so afraid of failing that he simply never even tried. He was so afraid to reach for the brass ring that he wasted his life away in a butcher shop that he loathed. He had given up his dreams because of this fear, and now I realized he couldn't even bear to watch his own son take the risks he had so desperately avoided.

Like so many others in our society, my father had been so paralyzed by his fears that he had actually convinced himself that anything, even giving up, was a better choice than risking. He was so blinded by this fear that even on his deathbed, he could not see that all my fearless risk-taking had paid off, that the reward for courage is the life of your dreams! But that fear was so powerful and so controlling that the success I had achieved was *invisible* to my own father. To my father, no dream, no matter how wonderful, was worth the pain to get there.

My father was no liberal. Far from it! But he shared one bad trait with Liberal Democrats. Liberals "feel your pain"—and they're terrified of it! They have the same character flaw as my father. They are so paralyzed and petrified by fear of pain that they are blind to the whole point of life. *Only through pain and failure can you grow.* You cannot (and should not) make the pain go away. To the contrary, it is necessary to learn, to grow, to succeed. If you eliminate the pain (or the risk), it stunts the growth.

Liberals mean well. But the road to hell is paved with good intentions! Liberals want to "save" society. They want to sanitize life. They are desperate to make the pain go away, to make everyone "safe." So what do they do? They force-feed us the ultimate narcotic—security (their beloved "safety net"). They can't see that life is contrarian. What appears to be "safe" is actually damaging and deadly. Safety destroys drive and ambition. Safety dulls creativity and enthusiasm. Safety damages dreams. Safety dumbs down the expectations of those it touches, takes away the edge of competitiveness. It induces complacency, laziness, and lowered expectations. Perhaps worst of all, safety renders personal responsibility DOA (dead on arrival). Those who offer safety nets have done no one a favor. The safety net provides safety, all right—few starve to death in America—but liberals don't realize that living in a hopeless coma is *worse* than death. The security of the safety net sucks the life out of everyone who accepts it. Without pain, there is no gain. Liberals miss the sad reality that living in a permanent state of coma is not a life worth living.

Life is meant to be lived, not feared. Risk and failure aren't bad, they are learning experiences. You either learn from them and use those lessons to go on and conquer your demons, or you curl up in a fetal position and die (maybe not physically, but emotionally, mentally, and financially). Success is all about learning to manage stress and become comfortable with risk. Those who never learn these traits are destined to spend their lives hiding under the covers or watching Jerry Springer, Jenny Jones, and soap operas (and TV ads for personal injury lawyers that air during shows like this). They spend their lives praying they keep their "safe" job and mediocre paycheck. They spend lives of quiet desperation in mental health clinics and government aid offices. Everyone has a choice between living and thriving or settling and surviving. Millionaire Republicans know that choosing security is settling for mediocrity, a choice my father had unwittingly made, a choice liberals make for others every day. It's the mistake of a lifetime.

There, at my father's bedside, I realized why so many individuals never get to experience the sweet smell of success. First you must have fire in your belly. You must be willing to risk, to fight with passion and abandon for your dreams. You've got to face challenges with daring and courage. You've got to be willing to feel the pain. You will find it is good for you in the long run. Liberals ignore the long run. They want to help people in pain right now (they feel your pain—unfortunately they're often the ones *causing* it). It's called "instant gratification." But now is temporary. To fix the pain now, to protect those in pain, to create artificial security, just cripples them in the long run. People need to experience pain. That's how you get stronger. Fire is required to turn iron into steel. To succeed, to thrive, you *must* risk. There is no reward without risk. Reward comes to those who choose to explore new frontiers and conquer their fears. Reward comes to those who go it alone without a government safety net and without a "safe" paycheck. Reward comes to those willing to put it all on the line, to personally guarantee the lease you need to start your new business, to put your life savings into that new business, to risk your home and assets on a dream, to quit your "safe" job to turn your dreams to reality. Rewards go to the big risk-takers, the big dreamers, the daring entrepreneurs, inventors, and creators—the "rainmakers." Rewards come to those who think and act like Millionaire Republicans. To those who believe "If it is to be, it is up to me." To those with faith. To those who truly believe that they can change the world—but only if government stays *out* of the way!

There is one more thing that I must share with you about my dad. Yes, he was a blue-collar butcher. Yes, he was a sur-

vivor, not a thriver. But that's not the full story, because my father was unique. He gave me a heck of a foundation in life, despite his fears. My father was one of a kind—a card-carrying
Republican butcher! He wasn't jealous of the success of others. He
did not support taxing others to redistribute wealth. No, he
never amassed a fortune or built a Fortune 500 company, but
he did eventually open his own butcher store. It was tiny, but it
was *his.* Even with all his fears and shortcomings, one man
made his own personal American Dream come true. He never
became a millionaire, but toward the end of his life, he was his
own boss. He fought his way from employee with a "safe" paycheck to independent small businessman. That was his small
dream, and he made it happen. My father, David Root, is a real-
life example of the type of independent thinkers that make up
the Republican Party. That tiny butcher store was never a financial success, but my father was still filled with pride and
hope—pride that he now *owned* something, that he was the boss
and answered to no one, and hope for his children. He knew
that in America, if you're smart and patient, success comes to
the *next* generation. He put all his hopes into me. He knew his
son would be special, and he told me so almost every day of my
life. That tiny butcher store never made David Root a rich man.
But it somehow paid for an Ivy League education for both of his
children. Only a Republican butcher could find a way to send
both of his children to Columbia University!

My sister, Lori, the daughter of the butcher, went on to
graduate from Columbia University and Columbia Law School.

She is today an attorney practicing in New York. I became an entrepreneur, TV celebrity, and Millionaire Republican. That butcher store never gave David Root all his dreams, but it opened the doors for his two children. My father sacrificed everything so his children could have it all. He gave up his dreams so we could live ours. He may not have achieved success in the classic sense of the word, but he sure *understood* it. And he never stopped believing, as he told me again and again: "The Republican Party is *not* the party of the rich, son. It's the party of anyone who *wants* to be rich. It is the party of dreams, of hope, of opportunity. The GOP is your ticket to a better life. Learn the principles of Millionaire Republicans—practice them, taste them, breathe them—and one day you too will live the American Dream."

Ironically, the blue-collar butcher from the tough streets of Brownsville, Brooklyn, understood success after all. He understood that it all starts with a foundation: faith. Faith in God and faith in your God-given talents. Faith in America and the limitless opportunities it offers. Faith in success that you must dream, taste, touch, and smell—*before* it ever happens. Faith in a future you cannot see, but that you know with every fiber of your being is waiting for you! David Root had faith in his children. And oh, how he had faith in his Republican Party, the party of opportunity and dreams. He believed, as all Republicans believe, that anything is possible in America for anyone—even an S.O.B. There are no excuses, no limitations as long as you work hard, take personal responsibility, educate yourself, fight with passion, and ask for nothing from government (except that it get out of your way). But you have to be willing to put it all on the line and risk courageously (once again, that's where *faith* comes in). Faith is truly the cornerstone of success. If you have that faith, if you're looking for that faith, this book is for you.

My father handed me an amazing foundation in life, and I ran with it. And I've never stopped running. The poor Republican butcher from Brooklyn believed that his son would make it big in America by faithfully following the principles and habits of rich Republicans. And he was right on the money. This book is dedicated to David Root. As he looks down from heaven now, I hope he understands that he is the very definition of a wealthy man! In the end, his dreams *were* fulfilled—because he led his children to the American Dream.

· 4 ·

My Story

CONFESSIONS OF A
MILLIONAIRE REPUBLICAN

Only those who dare to fail greatly can ever achieve greatly.

—ROBERT F. KENNEDY

I have a confession to make: I'm a Riverboat Gambler. You know, the kind of character that James Garner and Mel Gibson played in that Western movie *Maverick*. But that's not unusual. Almost all Millionaire Republicans are mavericks! We're dreamers, visionaries, independent thinkers, Riverboat Gamblers—at least gamblers in the business sense. We take risks. We put our money (and assets) where our mouths (and ideas) are! The process of taking risks, failing, picking yourself back up, and risking again is the hallmark of a Millionaire Republican. We aren't afraid of failing. As a matter of fact, we understand that failing is a natural part of the path to success. I call this philosophy *The Joy of Failure* (which is also the title of my second book, published back in 1997). I actually admit to failing my way to the top—heck, I based a book on it! Yes, I've failed literally thousands of times. But the key to my going from S.O.B. (Son of a Butcher) to Millionaire Republican is that between all the failures and rejections, I managed to hit a few balls out of the ballpark. That's the key. It only takes one big hit to strike it rich. Entrepreneurs (who are almost always Millionaire Republicans) have always understood that philosophy. Because attaining wealth is all about overcoming rejection and failure, most millionaires you'll meet are either in the sales business or run their own business. Entrepreneurs and salespersons have a unique mind-set—they understand that it only takes one *yes* to erase all the *no's* (even if it's thousands of *no's*) and that that one *yes* will change your life. Most (if not all) of the millionaires I know have struck out far more often than they've succeeded. But you're probably only aware of their one big hit, the grand-slam home run that put them on the map and into the pages of *Forbes, Fortune,* the *Wall Street Journal,* or on CNBC. (I've been featured or quoted in all four—sorry, I just couldn't resist telling you that.) That one big hit renders all the failures meaningless. That's the one big hit you'll be remembered for until the day you die (and maybe even after). All the *no's* are thankfully forgotten. *One* yes *changes your life!*

But success is about more than a willingness to risk (and sometimes fail). Success requires *action.* Millionaire Republicans understand that you cannot wait for opportunity to knock on your door. The biggest myth of all time is the one that says "Opportunity only knocks once." What a lie. The truth is that opportunity never knocks at all! You have to seek out opportunity—or, better yet, like a magician create it out of thin air. And once you find or create opportunity, you've got to knock it down, club it on the head, capture it, tie it up, and drag it home like a caveman! Creating wealth is not for the timid or the faint of heart. It is not a delicate or dainty process. It's a war out there! Trust me, nothing comes easy in the real world. It's a daily battle, and only the fittest survive—or should I say *thrive*! I'm proud to say that I'm a caveman—because the alternative is to lead a mediocre life, trapped in a "safe" job with a mediocre paycheck. You don't need to be a caveman for that kind of life. You don't need to be aggressive. You don't have to be action-oriented or goal-oriented. Anyone can have that kind of life. The question is "Who'd want it?" If you wanted it, you wouldn't be reading this book.

In this chapter, I'll tell you my story. The fakers and BS artists out there would try to con you into believing success is easy, or that they are so smart that they made it look easy. I won't insult you with drivel like that. This is the *true story* of how success and wealth are achieved in the real world. This is the story my father couldn't bear to hear: too much risk, too much failure, too much rejection and pain for his taste. But even more than that, it is the story of how I overcame my own fear of failure—again and again and again and again (ad nauseam). Buckle up and get ready for a wild ride!

I've repeatedly risked everything I have in order to succeed—and that's just in my own personal and business lives.

I'm not even talking about the 50,000 sports predictions and the 20,000 losses I've experienced in my career as a professional sports handicapper. Professional gamblers and handicappers like me understand the odds: winning 55 to 60 percent of the time is fantastic. You can earn millions of dollars with that kind of winning percentage. Yet that means you're going to lose a lot—at least four out of every ten gambles! Right there that adds up to 20,000 losses during my twenty-year career.

But we'll disregard those. Let's just consider my serious business failures. Before I ever became a professional sports prognosticator and before I even turned twenty-five, I had failed more than a dozen times. I tried my hand at a legal career but was rejected for law school; then I tried my hand at politics, but I lost my first political election at age twenty-one. I pursued careers as a real estate broker, a Wall Street stockbroker, a restaurant manager, a personal fitness trainer, and as the owner of numerous businesses—including a flower business, a commercial cleaning business, a nightclub, and a dating service. I failed miserably at all of them.

At this point, after all this risking, failing, and flailing, I was deep in debt and living at home with my parents. But I did have one thing going for me—I understood, even at that young age, that the key to success is *passion*. If you don't love what you do, the odds of being the best at it are between slim and none. So I just kept risking (and failing) until I found something that worked, something that made me feel that passion.

It was at this point in my life that I got a major break. I was having dinner with Douglas Miller, a businessman I had been introduced to as a possible investor in one of my many entrepreneurial ventures. Doug was a distinguished corporate CEO, and has since become my lifelong best friend, mentor, and business partner (and assisted me in writing and editing the book you are reading right now). Older, wiser, and experienced in the ways of business and of life, Doug took pity on me. He had no interest in my business proposals but, to my good fortune, took an interest in my career. He asked me a series of crucial questions: What did I want out of life? What were my specific goals? How would I get there? What was my game plan? (Did I even have a game plan?) It was out of this discussion between two new friends that my dream began to take shape.

Doug believed that success was tied to a straightforward three-step process. Step One, *"Establish your goals."* He asked me to "dream with him," and he asked me: "What do you really love doing? What gets you excited? What are your dreams? What are you passionate about?"

What is it that I really love doing? Now, that was an interesting question! I knew that I loved sports, specifically football. I also knew that I loved to gamble on sports. Growing up on the rough-and-tumble streets of New York, I'd been gambling on football since the age of thirteen. I also knew that I loved *talking* about both gambling and sports. I realized at that moment that if I could do anything in the world, I would predict the winners of major sporting events on national television.

So I turned to Doug and told him, "I love sports. I really like to gamble. And I think I'd be good at talking about it on television. I want to be my generation's Jimmy the Greek." At that time, Jimmy "The Greek" Snyder was America's most famous football prognosticator, starring on NFL pre-game shows on CBS. (And although the NFL will never admit it, the interest he helped create in betting on football was a major factor in making NFL football into America's number-one sport.) But at that time The Greek was getting old and would certainly retire (or be put out to pasture) soon.

Once I said it out loud, I knew that was it! This was the dream of my life. And, to my amazement, Doug agreed. I always say he was the first adult I ever told that crazy story to who didn't immediately say "You're out of your mind!"

"All right," he said. "Now you've told me your dream. One thing life has taught me is that the way you turn dreams into goals is by having a plan. You may or may not make your dream come true. But with a plan, you've got a chance. You are taking action and not just waiting around and hoping."

So, having a plan was Step Two in Doug's three-step success process. Given the formidable obstacles that stood in my way, developing a workable plan was not going to be easy. I had no money. I had no experience or education in the field I decided I was going to conquer. I'd never even taken a single broadcast journalism class in my life. I'd never spent *five minutes* in front of a television camera. And as for connections, my father was a butcher. If I wanted a nice piece of corned beef or bologna, I was hitting on all cylinders. But as far as knowing news directors or producers at major television networks, I was starting from ground zero.

But I was not daunted. And now that I had decided what it was that I wanted, I was not about to be stopped by a few seemingly insurmountable obstacles. So we put together a plan that literally put the odds in my favor. Our plan: attack, attack, and attack *aggressively.* I had no idea how much rejection and failure I was about to experience. I could never have imagined that all the failing I had experienced to this point would seem easy compared to what lay ahead. It's a good thing that I didn't comprehend the difficulty of the journey I was about to begin. If I had, I may not have tried!

That brings us to Doug's Step Three: implement, analyze, learn, change the plan, and implement again. We agreed that the first thing I needed was a bit of self-promotion. I needed to get my name on the map. I started by writing and printing a fancy brochure describing my talents and credentials as the Jimmy the Greek of my generation. I sent out five hundred of these brochures to radio, TV, and print media outlets, touting Wayne Allyn Root as the "greatest sports prognosticator in the world." Doug and I believed that attracting the attention of the press would be my best plan of attack. Five hundred brochures and press releases went out. *Not one single bite*—only five hundred rejections. Oh, but we did get one piece of helpful advice:

The receptionist for a TV producer called to inform us that we'd spelled Jimmy "The Greek" Snyder's name incorrectly. Great start!

So I sent out five hundred more brochures and this time followed up with phone calls. The response this time was much better—499 rejections, but *one* bite. A small local paper in Westchester County, New York, ran a story on my budding career. They called me the new Jimmy the Greek. They even contacted The Greek himself and asked him what he thought of my chances to succeed. Jimmy said, and I quote, "Tell this Root guy that in every town, village, and city in America, there are 500 guys lined up to become The Greek. Get in line!"

Back to the salt mines. Photocopy the article. Hey, it was the first time I could point to *someone else* saying something nice about my career, instead of just me. Type a new press release. Lick and seal. Send out five hundred copies again. No response, equaling five hundred rejections. Send out five hundred more. Four hundred and ninety-nine rejections, but once again, *one* bite. And this time I hooked a whale. The New York *Daily News,* at the time (1986) the largest urban newspaper in America, ran a full-page story in the sports section on "Wayne Root: The Sports Prognosticator of the Miami Vice Generation."

It was the break I needed. I was determined not to let it slip away. I begged, pleaded, and cajoled fifty of my nearest and dearest friends and relatives to write laudatory letters to the *Daily News* sports editor about Wayne Root. Of course, I coached them a bit on what to say—"What a story! We want to see more of Wayne Root" was how most of the letters started.

Within two weeks, the phone rang. It was the *Daily News* reporter, Filip Bondy, asking for another interview. "My editor has never received so many letters about a story before, so we'd like to do a follow-up." Once again, as soon as the article was printed in the *Daily News,* I went back to work. Fifty more letters from friends and family were sent to the editor demanding to see Wayne Root on a regular basis. Two weeks later, the phone rang again. This time it was the *Daily News* sports editor, Vic Zeigel himself, offering me my own column!

Now, terming it a "column" might be considered a slight exaggeration—it was actually a three-by-four-inch box that contained my NFL predictions each Sunday. They called me "The Yuppie Wonder." My pay? A whopping $50 per week. I remember Doug negotiating *hard* for that $50. I believe Vic's initial offer was for $40 per week. We won! Hey, it wasn't much, but it was a start. It may have only been a box, but it was *my* box. It had a byline with my name on it and more than a million New Yorkers could read it. That tiny box changed my life!

Back to the copy machine. I made hundreds of copies of my first column, along with a press release announcing that "Wayne Root, the world's greatest sports prognosticator, is hired by America's largest newspaper." Once again, I received hundreds of rejections but one yes. Are you starting to see a pattern here? No risk, no success. Hundreds of rejections and failures are meaningless. But one yes can change your life. The key to achieving the life of your dreams is taking the risks necessary to find that one yes! This time the one yes was from NBC radio in New York. I was offered a job predicting NFL winners on the popular *Joey Reynolds Show* each Friday afternoon.

The pay was even worse than it was at the *Daily News*: nothing! But the show offered me more exposure, more credibility, and, of course, the opportunity for more press releases! Once again, I was busy writing and sending out releases: "NY Daily News Prognosticator Root Joins NBC Radio." For a guy earning a grand total of $50 per week, I sure *sounded* impressive!

Looking back now, it seems ridiculous. I was a married man with a dream, living in a small bedroom in my parents' house, earning $50 a week and building a mountain of debt to publicize my career. But I had the right attitude, high hopes, lots of energy, and tons of unbridled enthusiasm. I was implementing the plan that made my dream an attainable goal. I knew that if I just didn't give up, I could make it happen. I was in constant motion and things were happening. It was the most exciting time of my life. As broke as I was, I don't think I've ever had more fun!

My NBC press release paid off. Within a few weeks, NBC radio in Chicago called. Would I be willing to predict football winners on *The Jonathon Brandmeier Show,* the number-one morning show in Chicago? This was not a tough decision.

The pay was par for the course: zero. But you couldn't beat the exposure! I knew I had another stepping-stone in my journey and another press-release headline! At this point, I now had over a million listeners in New York, over a million listeners in Chicago, and over a million New York readers. *I was a miniconglomerate, yet my combined income was still $50 per week!* My debts were escalating, but so was my career!

The great secret of success in life is for a man to be ready when his opportunity comes.

—BENJAMIN DISRAELI

I was on NBC Chicago for only a few short weeks before opportunity came knocking—loudly. Radio host Jonathon Brandmeier asked me to predict the outcome of a big ABC *Monday Night Football* game between his hometown Chicago Bears and the San Francisco 49ers. When I predicted a 49ers rout, Brandmeier came to the defense of his hometown heroes, suggesting (live on the air) that I was being rather foolish and shortsighted, "biting the hand that feeds me." He went on to suggest that the entire city of Chicago would publicly humiliate me if I was wrong.

I immediately sensed an opportunity to turn this disagreement into a major opportunity. I responded, "I'll take a chance on public humiliation, if you will too. Do I smell a bet?"

Brandmeier took the bait. He suggested, totally unrehearsed, that we devise a unique punishment for the loser of this bet. With the city of Chicago listening, he decided that if I was wrong about his beloved Bears on Monday night, I'd have to fly to Chicago to cohost his show in my underwear, outdoors, in the midst of a freezing Chicago December morning, in front of a crowd of hundreds of his screaming, taunting Chicago listeners. Now, that's public humiliation! But to me, it was only the opportunity for more publicity and more headlines. This bet was a "sure thing" that couldn't help but supercharge my career. Besides, when you're living on $50 a week, you've got to take a few chances!

Without missing a beat, I accepted and asked him if he'd be willing to do the same. He agreed that if he lost, he'd fly to New York to host his show in *his* underwear, outdoors, on a frigid New York December morning, in front of the world-famous Rockefeller Plaza. And he agreed that I'd be right by his side, co-hosting the festivities. The bet was agreed to, live on the air. My San Francisco 49ers won by one of the most lopsided scores in *Monday Night Football* history, 41–0.

Brandmeier flew to New York to host his radio show live from Rockefeller Plaza. True to his word, he stripped down to his polka-dot boxer shorts and appeared outside in ten-degree weather, with me by his side. He figured he'd have a little fun, amuse his listeners back home, and gain a few headlines for himself in both New York and Chicago. What he hadn't counted on was my ability to turn his appearance into a major media event for *me*. Remember, by this time I was pretty good at self-promotion!

I sensed an opportunity to take my career to a new level. Remember what I said earlier in the book about seizing opportunity? I emptied my bank account of my entire life savings, a grand total of a few thousand dollars, and hired a major New York public-relations firm to publicize the event. When Johnny B. stepped outside Rockefeller Plaza in his skivvies, he was met by dozens of news organizations from around the country: UPI, AP, *Entertainment Tonight,* all the TV tabloids, newspaper photographers, television cameramen, and reporters from virtually every TV news channel in New York. I had created an event! And, since it was my PR firm that was directing the event, I was the star! Headlines that night on every New York newscast sounded like this: "Chicago's biggest radio host hit town today, stripped of his clothes and his pride by famous New York sports prognosticator Wayne Root!" One newscaster reported, "It's easy to tell which one is Mr. Root and which one is Mr. Brandmeier. Root is the sharp-dressed New Yorker, smiling and looking like a winner. Brandmeier's the guy standing in the freezing cold without his pants!"

Overnight, I had made a name for myself! I was identified as a "winner" and a "famous New Yorker." Only hours before, I had been a broke nobody, living in my parents' house, working for $50 per week! I will always owe a debt of gratitude to Johnny Brandmeier, truly a man of his word. Thank you, Johnny!

The next day my phone rang. It was an executive at the NBC Source Radio Network, a group of over one hundred NBC radio stations appealing to young adult listeners. A group of NBC radio executives had been in the audience outside Rockefeller Plaza and watched me ham it up in front of the cameras with Johnny B. One of these executives was Stephen Soule, president of NBC Source Radio. Soule liked what he saw and offered me a job as a sports talk show host on more than one hundred NBC radio stations coast to coast. I was offered a fat salary, not to mention a limousine to and from the radio station. My life had just changed dramatically. Yet my days of risking and failing were not over—not by a long shot.

For several months I was limo'd to and from my NBC radio job. In between I was flown around the country to make publicity appearances at various NBC radio stations. I was given the star treatment wherever I went. My parents and my wife were incredulous. They had always suspected I was insane. Now they understood that there was a method to my madness!

Unfortunately, my bubble was about to burst. NBC unexpectedly announced the signing of *America's Top 40* radio superstar Casey Kasem to a multimillion-dollar contract. NBC executives hastily explained to me that those millions had to come from somewhere, and that my entire department was being cut. That meant I was terminated only three months after I had started. Well, as they say, "Easy come, easy go!" I had gone from the outhouse to the penthouse and back to the outhouse again in only a few months. But all wasn't lost. Even though my job was axed, I had a contract with NBC Radio that meant they had to pay me for a few more months. The way I looked at things (the eternal optimist), that meant I had *lots* of money to promote my career. I wasn't through—I was just getting started!

I knew television was my ultimate goal, so I took my NBC Radio income and produced a TV highlight tape at a professional studio. I then acquired a list of every local television station and national cable network in America and began sending out tapes via Federal Express, figuring that executive producers and news directors would stop and take notice of a FedEx package, that it would stand out from the crowd of packages and papers on their desk.

Unfortunately, the only things that stood out were my bills for overnight shipping, copies, stationery, business cards, video production, messengers, and follow-up phone calls to all corners of the country. I was eating up my entire NBC salary and then some! My debts were growing faster than my career—unfortunately, much faster!

The frustrating thing was that all that money I was spending wasn't paying off. The responses I got were more than just negative, they were downright humiliating. Mostly I heard deafening silence. Very few producers or TV executives would even take my follow-up phone calls. The few that did either said, "Don't call us again. If we're interested, we'll call you," or, "I've seen your résumé. You have no experience and didn't even graduate from broadcast or journalism school. You have no chance in this business. Stop wasting your time and ours." Then there was the *really* thoughtful response: "I watched your highlight tape. It was amateurish and unprofessional. Why don't you quit before you humiliate yourself further?"

It was at this time that I decided I needed a good agent. I was getting nowhere representing myself. Unfortunately, my search for an agent met with more rejection. I was rejected by every agent in the sports, news, and entertainment businesses. No decent professional would even consider representing someone as raw and inexperienced as I was.

At the time, my only choice was to pose as my own agent. Doug Miller had been continuing to mentor me, providing advice and encouragement. With his permission, I began making calls as "Wayne's agent," using Doug's name. The humiliations continued unabated. Of the hundreds of rejections that I received over the next few months while acting as my own agent, one stood out above all others. I still remember it like it was yesterday. An ABC-TV producer actually called upon receiving my tape. He said: "Your client Wayne Root is a joke. Hell will freeze over before this guy ever gets a job on television!" Of course, he didn't know he was talking directly to *me*. Ouch!

Looking back, this was one of the low points (but certainly not the only one) of my long journey. It was also one of the many occasions when I came close to deciding to give up my dream. At this point, the odds looked more than long, they looked downright impossible. However, each time that I considered giving up, some little victory materialized to keep me going. My tapes weren't exactly lighting up the television world, but those same promotional and video materials were attracting interest from investors. I was given the opportunity to start a business where I'd offer my predictions to sports bet-tors for a fee. I raised $150,000 and started a sports handicapping business called Pure Profit, Inc. My goals were simple: stay active, stay visible, keep fighting, and keep moving forward. After all, I kept hearing from Doug that it was impossible to fail if I just kept going. I hoped the exposure would lead to the TV career I coveted. Unfortunately, Pure Profit was *pure debt*. The business closed. Add just one more failure to the long list!

At this point, my long series of failures was beginning to take its toll. I didn't have a dime in the bank and my personal debts were approaching $150,000. That was a lot of money in 1988, especially when my weekly income was $50. It was soon after this last disaster that I was forced to declare personal bankruptcy. Within months, my first marriage was over as well. My wife announced she was leaving me for another man. Ouch again!

I wasn't just failing, I was finding new and innovative ways to fail. And the failures seemed to be getting bigger, more expensive, and more painful. But an aspiring Millionaire Republican doesn't give up or hide under the covers. I trudged forward and risked some more. Risk creates opportunity, or so I hoped and prayed!

Just as I hit rock bottom, I was saved again. My business may have been "out of business," my television career going nowhere, my marriage in shambles, and my bank accounts busted, but my nonstop promotions and press releases were paying off. Bantam Books, one of America's largest and most prestigious publishers, agreed to publish my first book, *Root on Risk: Betting to Win on Sports.* It was a small and short-lived moral victory. They never promoted the book, and it was a flop. Add one more failure to the long list.

But being a published author opened up another door for me. The *Robb Report* magazine gave me a job as a contributing sports editor. The *Robb* is like a toy store for the world's wealthiest men and women. I read it religiously back then and still do today, always using it as a motivational tool (visualizing the life I want to live). The average Robb reader earns almost a million dollars per year. My name was positioned in front of the movers and shakers of the business world. I was able to interview many of the biggest names in sports: Mark Spitz, Bruce Jenner, Mario Andretti, Lyle Alzado, Steve Garvey, Dallas Cowboys owner Jerry Jones, and the commissioners of the NBA, NFL, and PGA. Despite setback after setback, I was making a name for myself, gaining credibility, and most important, *I was staying in the game.* I was literally risking and failing my way to the top!

I was also attracting the attention of some major television networks. First, I was called by Bill MacPhail, the legendary boss of CNN Sports. He had an opening for a sportscaster at CNN, and I was on his short list. I immediately flew to Atlanta to audition for the job. I didn't get it, but it was an honor to be considered. It gave me a boost of confidence and convinced me that my goal was within reach.

Within days of my return from Atlanta, FOX Television executive Michael Binkow called and invited me to fly to Los Angeles to interview for the host position of a new national television sports show. The show was aimed at a young, hip, urban audience, and Binkow made it clear that I fit the bill perfectly. I was so excited and sure that this was the break I'd been waiting for, I asked Doug to go with me as my agent, and I insisted on paying for his flight.

Once I got to Los Angeles, it became clear that this was just another false alarm. The show was merely at the "exploration stage." I would soon learn that in Hollywood, that's television-talk for "pipe dream." I had flown across the country for *nothing*. More money wasted, money that I didn't have, just another credit card debt that I couldn't pay. Here I was at perhaps the lowest point in my life, facing the abyss. Others would have quit. Some probably would have had suicidal thoughts from the humiliation. At the very least, most would have gone home and settled for a "real job" and a "safe" paycheck. I remained undaunted. Instead of getting discouraged, I grew more determined. Here I was with my "agent" in Los Angeles, all dressed up with no place to go.

The trip was already paid for, and I wasn't about to fly home with my tail between my legs. I decided we should start "dialing for dollars." We began dialing every television station in Los Angeles. I vowed to turn a wasted cross-country trip and the biggest disappointment of my young career into the biggest break of my life. And I did!

Doug and I sat in our hotel room for two full days dialing and waiting for the phone to ring. It never did. At one point even Doug, the eternal optimist, suggested giving up and heading back home. His exact words were, and we still laugh about this conversation to this day: "Wayne, it's one thing to be a positive thinker. It's another to be a glutton for punishment. You've got to know when to give up. You're humiliating yourself. Please stop. I can't stand seeing you put yourself through so much pain."

Instead of listening to reason, I was angered and inspired by Doug's words. I was an underdog with a chip on my shoulder. I made another dozen calls. Just like the old days, I experienced 99 percent rejections—but one bite, and it was a *big* one. After more than a year of effort and a dozen unanswered phone calls to Arnie Rosenthal, general manager of Financial News Network (FNN Sports), I decided I had nothing to lose by taking one more shot, to place one more call. Thank God that I'm a gambler! Lucky number thirteen changed my life forever.

I was shocked when *Rosenthal himself* actually got on the phone. "Where are you?" he asked. When I told him I was in Los Angeles, his response was like music to my ears: "Wow, what great timing. Our number-one anchorman, Todd Donoho, just announced this morning that he's leaving for ABC-TV. How soon can you be here?"

Doug and I probably set the cross-town speed record that day! Within an hour I found myself sitting in the executive offices of Financial News Network (now known as CNBC), negotiating a deal that would put me on national television in front of over 33 million viewers. We shook hands that day. I flew home to New York, told my family that I'd been hired by Financial News Network as an anchorman and TV host, packed my bags, got into my car, and drove cross-country to Los Angeles to start my new life.

I'll never forget it. I arrived in L.A. on a Wednesday. On Thursday I walked into my new office in the FNN newsroom. By Friday I was standing on the field at Dodger Stadium interviewing Tommy Lasorda! One day I was broke, living in a small bedroom in my parents' house, and a few days later I was living in a Hollywood Hills dream home overlooking the twinkling lights of Los Angeles, hanging out with Tommy Lasorda and the Dodgers. I had literally risked and failed and hustled and self-promoted my way to the top

But wait, it gets better. A few weeks later I was called into the general manager's office. When I walked in, Arnie Rosenthal said, "Wayne Root, meet your new cohost, Jimmy 'The Greek' Snyder." Talk about full circle! I had started all those many years and risks and rejections ago with a dream to become the new Jimmy the Greek, and now here I was standing next to the legend himself, talking about the plans for *our* new NFL pre-game show!

A couple of weeks later Arnie called me into his office again. He told me that I would spend the month of July flying across America to every NFL training camp to interview the biggest stars of football. When I returned, I'd start hosting my new NFL pre-game show with Jimmy the Greek. The kid that loved football and gambling was now going to get paid to interview NFL stars and talk football and gambling, all on national TV, on his *own* show, sitting next to Jimmy the Greek.

Was all that risk and rejection worth it? You're darn right it was! What is it that the fitness fanatics say? "Without pain, there is no gain." Well, I experienced plenty of pain, rejection, failure, divorce, humiliation (remember "Hell will freeze over before Wayne Root lands on TV"?), and bankruptcy. But now I was living the "gain." This S.O.B. was now a TV star! My crazy dream of talking about NFL football and sports gambling on TV was now my life. Millionaire Republican, here I come!

I had proven all the critics wrong. All the experts believed my dream was a joke—but the joke was on *them*. I risked and failed thousands of times. But none of the failures mattered. I found the one *yes* that changed my life. It had been quite a ride and quite a payoff at the end . . . except for one small detail. It *wasn't* the end. This was just the beginning.

After two years of hosting and anchoring, as well as picking NFL point-spread winners as FNN network prognosticator, I decided to take the biggest gamble of my life—yes, bigger than all the others combined! I decided to quit FNN to become a full-time professional sports handicapper.

How big was the risk? I had gone from bankrupt and living in my parents' home to popular national TV host. And now I was risking everything I had just achieved on a *new* gamble, a new dream! Anchorman and host had never been my dream, nor was collecting a weekly paycheck. I'm a Riverboat Gambler—always have been, always will be.

To me the "brass ring" was to earn my living as the most famous professional handicapper and gambler in America. My new short-term goal would be to turn my professional gambling advice into a business—a *big* business. So I left FNN to join a football handicapping show called *Proline* on the USA TV network. Even riskier, I went from earning an anchorman's salary to earning *no* salary. My new job was performance-based—I'd work strictly on commission, based on the revenues generated by my handicapping advice.

And what did the critics, including my friends and family, say this time around? Any encouragement? Anything positive? I heard:

"Are you out of your mind?"

"You're leaving a job as a TV host and anchor to become a professional gambler?"

"You're leaving Financial News Network for a gambling infomercial?"

"You're self-destructive. You must want to ruin your career."

"You're leaving a fat weekly paycheck and the security of a big TV network for a commission with no guarantee? You've gone nuts."

"You are really a reckless gambler."

The critics are always out there, looking to make you doubt yourself, looking to discourage you, depress you, destroy your confidence, and ruin your plans. One of my greatest strengths is that I never listen to critics. I just keep moving forward, making things happen, taking calculated risks to improve my life. And once again, the risk was worthwhile.

When I left Financial News Network to sell my sports handicapping advice on TV for a fee, few had ever heard of the fledgling 900-number telephone business. Those who had heard of it didn't think much of it. It sure was "risky." And it certainly didn't compare to the status of being an anchorman—or at least that's what my fellow anchormen and everyone else thought.

That, of course, was *before* I became a self-made millionaire by selling my handicapping picks to sports gamblers on TV. That was *before* I attracted over *one million* television callers paying $25, $50, and $100 per call for my advice. That was *before* I bought my first home on the beach in Malibu. I turned my winning gambling advice into big business—just as I predicted. (Hey, goals work!) Once again, I had risked and won big. Once again, I had proven my critics, naysayers, and detractors wrong—*dead wrong.*

But once again, this was a beginning rather than an end. The money was great for the next decade, but after a decade of success and more calls from American sports gamblers than any TV handicapper ever, I decided to risk again. I left *Proline* and the company that had turned me into a Millionaire Republican. I left behind a life that no normal person could imagine ever leaving, just as I had at FNN. I walked away from financial security. (The Las Vegas company that I worked for was the leader in the handicapping industry for over twenty years.) The job and the financial security it produced was mine for life—if I wanted it. But I wanted something more.

Even more than the money, I was leaving behind an amazing lifestyle. My job was to fly first-class to Las Vegas once a week, get picked up at the airport by a limo, be driven to a luxury suite at a four-star hotel, star on *Proline,* and then fly back first-class to my Malibu beachfront home. The rest of the week, I was paid to sit poolside at my Malibu estate watching football and counting my money. How many sane people in the world would risk *everything* to leave that life? Only a Millionaire Republican would! Because our goals are freedom, independence, mega-wealth, and unlimited success. And those are things you don't get by settling or standing pat. We're Riverboat Gamblers, and we understand that to *really* succeed, you have to roll the dice.

So, with a new baby (my first son, Hudson) on the way and a huge mortgage in Malibu (that beachfront lifestyle comes with a big price tag), I gave all that job security up. The Riverboat Gambler in me had a gut instinct again. It was time to start my own business. And it was time to take the biggest risk of my life—again. From this point on, nothing would be guaranteed. I had no idea how I'd finance my new business, I just knew that it would take millions of dollars to start. Was I scared? Of course I was! But I was willing to risk everything on my new dream (what else is new?): to be my own boss. No pain, no gain.

Now I wanted it *all*. I had started out with a crazy dream to become my generation's Jimmy the Greek—and against all odds, I'd succeeded. Next, I'd aimed for a starring role on national TV with no prior experience—and against all odds, I'd succeeded. Then I'd aimed to turn my unique prediction skills into a big business—and against all odds, I'd succeeded again. My new dream was to build my own sports handicapping business empire. My plan was to leave all my financial security behind, to create a TV show from ground zero, start a business from ground zero, become CEO as well as professional sports handicapper (despite never having been a CEO), and build my company (which did not yet even exist) into an industry leader that I could take public on Wall Street. I also planned to expand globally to predict the winners of soccer, cricket, and rugby events. Lofty goals! As always, Millionaire Republicans think big. We aim to make the impossible *possible*.

Instead of a huge guaranteed income, I walked away from my employer with nothing guaranteed except the risk of losing everything I had in this world. I invested my own money, and as a "bonus" put my home on the line as a financial guarantee. I turned to my mentor and friend of almost twenty years, Doug Miller, to be my business partner. Doug had spent his entire career as an entrepreneur. The very first thing he did was try to talk me out of it. He warned me that business start-ups are hell. He said we'd work 24/7 and there would be no such thing as weekends or holidays. He said that there would be days I'd curse my decision. He was right on all counts! But the payoff was that I'd be my own boss. It sounded good to me! This gambler was *all in.*

There was the problem, however, of those pesky critics again. The knives are always out, no matter what your status in life. My old boss had some interesting parting words of wisdom: "You'll *never* make it without me. You'll *never* make it without my money. You'll *never* make it without my TV show. What I built took me twenty-five years. You can't replicate it in *fifty*! You've got no chance."

The TV experts said, "You'll never get a sports handicapping show on TV." Other than *Proline,* there were no sports handicapping shows on national TV for a reason: television networks will not accept them. The financial experts said, "You'll never raise the money necessary to build this niche business from ground zero." I wanted to take my company public. Nobody believed I could do it. The Wall Street experts all said, "Are you joking? Sports handicapping, public? It will never happen!"

All these cynics, critics, and naysayers had been negative *before* the life of an entrepreneur got really tough—within weeks, the Internet revolution imploded and the stock market crashed (in April of 2000). I needed to raise millions of dollars to start my business, all with the stock market in the middle of its worst period since 1929. Venture capital dried up, and investors were nowhere to be found. The economy was plunging into a recession. I had burned my bridges with my old employer and could not go back. I was in the middle of a never-ending nightmare. So what happened? How did the "King of Risk" get himself out of this bind?

- The experts said I'd never raise the start-up money I needed to found GWIN. I was looking for $5 million, but I've wound up raising almost $20 million since the inception of GWIN.

- The experts said I'd never get a new football handicapping show approved on a national TV network. Over the past five years, I've gotten *Wayne Allyn Root's WinningEDGE* approved on four major national television networks: PAX, FOX SportsNet, Spike TV, and now Superstation WGN. Not only did the TV experts predict that a gambling-oriented sports show could not find a home on a major cable network, they were 100 percent certain that it would never gain approval on a TV network that broadcasted NFL games. With our launch on FOX SportsNet in 2002, the experts were proven dead wrong again!

- The experts said I'd never be able to create a high-quality television show—one that looked more like a network pre-game football show than a gambling show. I can see why they doubted me. As a handicapper, I'd never been behind the camera, never created a show from scratch, or played the role of executive producer. The critics, of course, were wrong again. (Are you starting to see a pattern here?) In our first year we hired Bob Levy, the director of the FOX Sports NFL Pre-Game show (starring Terry Bradshaw and Howie

Long) to direct our show. We designed a state-of-the-art TV set. We signed NFL Hall of Famers John Riggins, Randy White, and Dan Hampton, along with former New York Giants star Phil McConkey, to appear on the show alongside me. Over the last couple of years we've added two-time AFC Coach of the Year Ron Meyers, Sporting News Radio host and Emmy Award winner Chet Coppock, and nationally recognized handicapping champions Larry Ness and Al McMordie. I can state with pride that *Wayne Allyn Root's WinningEDGE* is the most watched sports handicapping show ever on American television.

- The experts said we'd never be able to take our company public on Wall Street. They were really certain of this one! Today, we are America's only publicly traded sports handicapping firm.

- The experts said sports handicapping had nothing in common with Wall Street. The company that we have created is modeled identically after a Wall Street brokerage firm. Our TV show is similar to *Wall Street Week,* with experts discussing and debating their favorite "investments." It's just a lot more fun to watch your investment run for a touchdown or sack the quarterback than it is to watch a portfolio full of IBM and Microsoft. The handicappers on my show are positioned just like the analysts at major mutual funds or hedge funds. Our clients call to speak to our sports brokers just as they speak to their stockbrokers on Wall Street. Our brokers sit in offices, complete with the latest computer and telemarketing equipment, looking just like a Merrill Lynch brokerage office. I've been quoted on *Wall Street Week* and Forbes.com, and profiled by *Fortune* magazine, CNBC, and the *Wall Street Journal.* And I've become a regular guest on CNBC, the business authority on American television. CNBC recently compared Wall Street to "Wayne's Street"! FOX News in Las Vegas recently reported that "Root's success is mind-blowing. . . . Wayne Allyn Root has built a one-man empire by applying the principles of Wall Street to sports gambling." All things considered, I'd say the company I created now has much in common with Wall Street.

- Another big goal for GWIN is about to be achieved as well. My goal from the first day that we founded GWIN was to become the *global* brand name in sports handicapping—to provide professional advice and analysis on international gambling sports like soccer, cricket, rugby, and Formula One racing. We are currently making plans to expand our operations globally, and not just handicapping—we have just announced plans to open Wayne Root online poker sites aimed at Asian and European gamblers. If Merrill Lynch can be global, then so can GWIN!

- And finally, one more crazy dream of mine has become a reality against all odds. I dreamed up a national television gaming competition with a $1 million winner-take-all prize, called *King of Vegas.* With the help of my longtime friend Michael Yudin, this major TV series is now a reality! On the very week I finished writing this book, Spike TV announced that *King of Vegas* will join their prime-time lineup in January 2006. The executive producers are Wayne Allyn Root, Michael Yudin, and Brian Gadinsky (formerly of *American Idol*). After thousands of hours of work and dozens of rejections and disappointments along the way, another risk has paid off, another dream has come true, another new career has begun.

I am not unique in my attitude—there are millions of Millionaire Republicans in this great country. You too can create that attitude, and with it that kind of mega-wealth and unlimited success. Millionaire Republicans are not born—they are self-made! As my mentor and business partner Doug Miller loves to say, "Everything is easy if you know what to do!" My goal in this book is to show you what to do and how to do it. My Millionaire Republican attitude about risking and failing has allowed me to succeed in the disparate worlds of television, gaming, business, publishing, and, hopefully, soon in politics as well. You can apply my philosophy and strategy to your own personal and business life. You too can morph from being just a survivor to being a *thriver;* from having a fear of failure to being a daring, courageous, risk-taking Riverboat Gambler; from being a renter to an owner; from being an S.O.B. to being a Millionaire Republican. But you must first "model" the right person— the *right* kind of millionaire. In the next chapter, you'll learn that not all millionaires are created equal.

· 5 ·

Not All Millionaires Are
Created Equal

THE LUCKY SPERM CLUB

I am opposed to millionaires, but it would be dangerous to offer me the position.

—MARK TWAIN

I told you that my father taught me that Step One in becoming a Millionaire Republican was to learn to think like one. So let's start by talking definitions. Not all millionaires are created equal. Looks can be deceiving. I graduated from Columbia University—one of the great Ivy League institutions of higher learning. And as an S.O.B., I felt lonely, isolated, rejected, out of place, primarily because *I was!* My classmates were the elite of the elite, the sons and daughters of privilege. Their parents had graduated from Columbia or Harvard or Princeton, and their brothers and sisters had graduate degrees from Harvard Law, Stanford medical school, and Wharton business school. So did their grandfathers. My dad, on the other hand, barely got out of high school. My maternal grandfather had come to America penniless. My paternal grandfather died in the poor ward of a Brooklyn hospital. Harvard degrees and law degrees were not in my genes. My Columbia classmates took family vacations to London, Paris, Rome, Gstaad, Sydney, St. Barts, Rio de Janeiro, and of course spent Christmas in Aspen. My family spent a week at a motel on the Jersey Shore each summer. Their fathers were prominent CEOs, political leaders, doctors, lawyers, investment bankers, Wall Street tycoons, diplomats, and business moguls. My dad wore a bloody white apron and cut meat for a living. Many of my classmates had trust funds waiting for them, or, if not trust funds, they certainly had Dad's money and connections to open every door. I had to work my way through college—and the rest of my life! They played golf, tennis, squash, rode horses, and skied like pros on the slopes of Aspen. I did not know how to do any of that. The only sports I played growing up on the mean streets of New York were Kill the Carrier and street football (with no helmets or pads). Yes, I was from a different planet.

Now, while some of their parents (or more likely grandparents) may have been Millionaire Republicans (as most self-made entrepreneurs are), these children of privilege were *not*. To the contrary, they were all extreme Liberal Democrats. Years later, when I began living the good life on the beach in Malibu, I was surrounded by the Hollywood elite. They were the cream of the crop: famous celebrities, movie moguls, agents, directors, producers, screenwriters—millionaires all. And they too were extreme Liberal Democrats. The point is, all millionaires are *not* created equal. All millionaires are certainly not Millionaire Republicans.

If your goal is to become a millionaire, and you're starting from ground zero, you must understand the difference between a Millionaire Republican and a Millionaire Democrat. For the most part, the only way you can replicate the success of a Millionaire Democrat is to start over again and choose different parents, or marry someone who happened to be born rich (after all, that's what they did!). But everyone has the potential to replicate the success of the *right* kind of millionaire—the Millionaire Republican.

When you are looking for millionaires to admire, listen to for advice, and model your life after, the primary thing that should matter to you is where a millionaire *starts* and how he or she got to the top. The big difference is that most of us Millionaire Republicans earned our way to the top with tenacity, determination, hard work, and chutzpah! To a man (or woman), rich Republicans are almost always self-made entrepreneurs and daring risk-takers. And the result is that we owe nothing to anyone—not to our daddies' money (although we love our parents); not to our bosses (we rarely have bosses—we have "partners" or own our own businesses); and certainly not to government—*especially* not to government.

What Millionaire Republicans all have in common is that

we found a way to beat the odds and surmount the obstacles. We created and seized opportunities that others did not even know were there. We were never afraid to fail—and because we took daring chances, we failed often. But we are fighters, and we never ever gave up! Eventually all that fighting, risking, failing, and daring dreaming worked out! Therefore we have no reason to feel guilt or shame, or that our success had to do with luck. Luck had nothing to do with it. We made our success happen the only way you can when you start with nothing—by following the 18 Republican Secrets of Mega-Wealth and Unlimited Success!

Building wealth and creating financial freedom in your life isn't an easy journey. If you think it's going to be easy, you might as well stop reading right now! In most cases, it's a rocky road, full of ups and downs, and with humbling failures that force you to start all over again. Earlier in the book you heard about just a few of my own. But that's okay—failure is a natural part of life and a critical component of success. Failures automatically happen when you are self-made and start with nothing. They are a natural part of the process. They even happen to those privileged kids I attended Columbia with. But let me tell you, failures are a whole lot easier to deal with, and it's a whole lot easier to start over again, when you have Daddy's money, country-club connections, and a huge trust fund behind you. It makes all the difference in the world!

With nothing to fall back on, Millionaire Republicans have developed a whole different mind-set. We believe in personal responsibility, limited government, low taxation, and the encouragement of wealth creation. We understand that success is fragile and therefore needs to be nurtured, encouraged, and rewarded. And we understand that that only happens with low taxes and limited government. We understand that lower taxes allow more Americans to save up the funds necessary to start a business or fund a daring venture. We understand that the fewer government bureaucrats, the better our chance for success. We are in a unique position to understand the American Dream and all its amazing possibilities—because we now live it (despite all the obstacles). We are living proof that capitalism works and that everyone has the potential to become a Millionaire Republican.

To listen to the "born rich" talk, you would think they're unaware that if it weren't for their rich connected parents they'd be struggling just like the rest of us. Or perhaps they *do* know and that's what causes them to suffer such immense guilt. Millionaire Republicans do not feel guilt! We *earned* our money and success and therefore have no reason to be guilty. Rich liberals didn't. But now they want us to play by the same rules. Heck, they want us to feel the same guilt! They want us to give away much of what we make in taxes to fund a welfare society and call it "fair." In reality, it's all a big sham. The spoiled-brat trust-fund crowd isn't for higher taxation to help those less fortunate. Quite the contrary, it's their way of keeping control, of staying at the top, of keeping the rest of us out of their clubs, of making sure they stay as the "haves," while the rest of us stay as part of the "have nots."

It is this simple: If successful, wealthy, self-made people like me have to pay the same taxes on income as the lucky-sperm-club, trust-fund, spoiled-brat, rich kids with all their connections, power, and wealth, guess who has all the advantages? Those of us not born to wealth are forced to pay huge taxes on the income on which we *live.* The result is that we do not have enough money left to start our businesses, fund our ideas, or buy stocks or real estate at an opportune moment in time. That is, after all, precisely how the rich stay rich and get richer. My privileged Columbia trust-fund classmates are only too happy to pay the same huge tax rates as me on their income. And why not? They don't live on their income! They have a $10 million trust fund, or the equivalent—Daddy's $10 million—behind them. The Kennedys and Heinz-Kerrys of the world could pay 90 percent taxes on earned income and it wouldn't mean a thing to them—they don't *live* on their income. They already have a billion dollars stashed in tax shelters. They already own multiple mansions all over the world (filled with servants). They already control billion-dollar companies. Taxes are for the "little people." Only the "working rich" pay them—self-made Millionaire Republicans like me, who rely on our income to live, to fund cash-flow problems at our businesses, to start new businesses, to buy stocks and real estate. Most self-made "working rich" entrepreneurs rarely have any savings for the first twenty years of our careers starting and growing companies. Live off interest? We don't have principal, let alone interest. Our money is too busy "working" to worry about interest!

If you work your fingers to the bone 24/7 to earn a six-figure income, you are precisely the kind of sucker that the trust-fund crowd thinks should pay those high rates of taxes. They want to punish you for getting "rich." Or, to put it in the correct terms, they want to punish you for having the *audacity* for thinking you could get as rich as them! This "benevolent" desire to raise taxes to supposedly help those less fortunate is actually a well-disguised, hypocritical sham to screw the working rich and self-made entrepreneurs of the world, and to keep those at the very top *alone* at the very top.

In a later chapter we'll look at the other side of taxes—the argument that we need high income taxes to help the "less fortunate." This may be the biggest hypocrisy of all! The objective of the Liberal Left is not redistributing income or helping those less fortunate. Their true objective is twofold: First, it's the one touched upon in the previous paragraph, but that can't be stressed enough. It is to use high tax rates to starve the bright, ambitious, hungry middle class looking to move up. Starve them of their working (and living) capital, so they can never quite get ahead. Force them to spend their lives living in quicksand, always slipping back due to lack of funds and "seed money" until they are finally broken and give up, ready to accept whatever the "benevolent" government and welfare state gives them. The second objective is even more insidious: using entitlements as a drug to keep the poor content yet hopeless, giving them just enough "incentive" (entitlements, welfare, food stamps, etc.) so that they're unwilling to fight the system and willing to stay poor (and keep voting Democrat, of course).

It's ironic that history proves that the one thing high taxes and a huge government welfare state don't do is help those less fortunate. History proves that people getting government handouts do not move up—they very often stay addicted to government handouts for life. Generation after generation is "hooked" on entitlements. Ambition and incentive are destroyed. The very groups that need the help most have not improved their standard of living in the fifty years since President Lyndon Johnson instituted his "Great Society" policies. Look around the ghettos of major American cities—nothing has changed in half a century. Entitlements have done their job, all right—they've kept the poor living in abject poverty!

· 6 ·

Modeling the *Right* Kind
of Millionaire

When I was young I used to think that money was the most important thing in life.

Now that I am old, I know it is.

—OSCAR WILDE

There's something that I think is important for you to know about this book. Yes, I'm a Millionaire Republican. If you want to be a Millionaire Republican as well, that fact should not intimidate you. As a matter of fact, it should inspire and motivate you. I'm not special and I wasn't born to the "right parents." The fact that I was able to achieve Millionaire Republican status means that you also have the potential to achieve it. Business success is all about "models." Find a model that works, and then *replicate* it. That's Business 101. Once you find a successful model to follow, all you need to do to succeed is work harder than your competition, innovate, aggressively create, and take advantage of opportunities. Most important, never ever, ever, ever, give up. That's my formula.

It's pretty darn simple. It's too bad they don't bother teaching that lesson in school. Since few (if any) teachers and academic bureaucrats are Millionaire Republicans, they keep busy by teaching our kids useless crap that dumbs them down. They are focused on training our children to settle for "security" and collect a measly mediocre paycheck, working at a job they will never truly love, for a boss they undoubtedly hate.

You can succeed by following my model no matter where you start in life. But let me warn you, replicating Donald Trump, Bill Gates, Warren Buffett, George Steinbrenner, Puffy Combs, Russell Simmons, Mark Cuban, Richard Branson, and other assorted billionaires or $500-million men, well, that's pretty intimidating. And it's also pretty *unrealistic*. No matter how smart, creative, or tenacious you are, the odds of you modeling a billionaire and succeeding are close to nil. I'm not a billionaire. I'm just a little old millionaire, and a relatively *small* one at that. Donald Trump can buy me a thousand times over. Between my company, my stocks, real estate, cash, etc., I have total assets of around $5 million at the age of forty-four. From where I started, that's pretty cool! And I'm far from done. By the time I hit retirement age (although I never plan to retire), I should be in the $20 million to $30 million range, minimum. Donald Trump would probably snicker at that amount of assets. That's "chump change" to him. It wouldn't pay for one of his mansions, the annual costs of maintaining and fueling his fleet of private jets and helicopters, or even the cost of the crew and fuel for his yacht. But my level of success and wealth is a *re-*

alistic target for you. In this great country, anyone can start with nothing and achieve my level of wealth in his or her lifetime.

When I was attending Columbia University, I took an economics class. Every few weeks the professor would bring in a guest lecturer to talk about their business success. The guest was always an impressive businessman or -woman who owned or served as CEO of a $100 million company. They were all dynamic business tycoons and celebrated moguls direct from the pages of *Forbes, Fortune,* and the *Wall Street Journal.* Their talks were invariably about how they had started from scratch, struggled, overcome hurdle after hurdle, and were now hugely successful. You could literally see the awe in the eyes of my classmates. Then the lecture would end and the speaker would open the floor to questions from the audience. My hand always shot up first. And my question was always the same: "Where did you get the initial capital to start this amazing, remarkable, stunningly successful multimillion-dollar business?" Ninety percent of the time the answer was some variation of "Well, my dad did countersign a $10 million loan for me," or "It was my father's business that I took over," or "My grandfather was the original founding partner of the firm I now run." Upon hearing that answer, my response was always the same: I'd get up and walk out of the class. After all, there was nothing more for me to learn. My experience could never be the same as that speaker's experience. We came from *different* worlds. We started in far different places and circumstances. Our experiences were so different, we might as well have been from different planets. I couldn't hope to replicate their success because without the rich daddy, it just wasn't possible.

As much as I admire Donald Trump's chutzpah and dynamic style, or Bill Gates's genius, I feel the same way about their books as I do the books of most big-shot business moguls: The books and the wisdom in them are *useless* to you if you didn't start out with the same trust fund, connections, or business inherited from daddy. The success of billionaire big shots who started out in the Lucky Sperm Club is a mirage to us mere mortals. You *think* you can see that kind of superhuman success in your future, but you can't ever reach it—not without the same rich daddy and spectacular start in life. The other reason these books are useless to you is simply that the main reason these big-shot CEOs got their book deals in the first place is because they have achieved such awe-inspiring and one-in-a-billion levels of success. But those levels are so rare that they are unrealistic models, and it's counterproductive to try to follow them. Their kind of success is so off the charts that you can never replicate it. Worse, it's depressing and intimidating to even try. When you see where billionaires like Gates and Trump are today and compare it to where you are, it rarely inspires. To the contrary—it makes you feel inferior. After reading about their remarkable exploits and achievements, success seems so far out of reach, why even try?

Let me give you just a little taste of how things are *not* always as they seem with the billionaire business moguls you admire. I know I will be accused of jealousy and sour grapes. Not true.

This Millionaire Republican values and respects the success of billionaires like Trump and Gates. Both are among the greatest business legends in history. But there are still lessons to be learned here. It's valuable for you to keep in mind the kind of families that Donald Trump and Bill Gates were fortunate enough to be born into.

Most people think (because that's the way "The Donald" wants us to think) that Donald Trump made it all happen through sheer smarts, willpower, and talent. But there are a few select facts missing in *The Apprentice* star's story: the great marketing genius, world-class self-promoter, and self-proclaimed "self-made billionaire" had a nice start that you'll never have. You see, his daddy, Fred Trump, was one of the biggest developers and owners of apartment buildings in Brooklyn and the outer boroughs of New York *before* Donald was even born! Mr. Self-Made had a family fortune of a reported $400 million *before* he ever started his amazing real estate career. And that was when $400 million was real money! Not a bad start! As a matter of fact, if Donald had failed miserably and *lost* half his family's fortune, he'd still be a fabulously wealthy $200-million man! Now, that's my kind of choice. On the day of your birth, behind door number one, is $400 million. Behind door number two, in the event that you screw up, is $200 million. And behind door number three, if you're smart and work hard (which I'll certainly give Trump massive credit for doing), is *billions.* But those three choices were only there because he had daddy's wealth, connections, and know-how to grow that $400 million start!

And by the way, another little thing: the connections he inherited were worth *far* more than the money.

"The Donald" was in his twenties when he got hundred-million-dollar real estate loans to start his career. Could you or I get a loan like that? As a Son of a Butcher, my connections could get me a nice piece of bologna. My family heritage was a cramped, freezing butcher store with two butcher blocks, bloody aprons, and sawdust on the floor. I will venture to guess that you come from a background closer to mine than to Trump's.

Then there's Bill Gates. Yes, the King of Microsoft is a brilliant businessman, perhaps one of the brightest ever. But he too had a few breaks in life. He may be the richest man in the world today, but he was in pretty good shape on his day of birth, too! You see, Bill picked the perfect parents. His father, Bill Gates Sr., was one of the wealthiest and most powerful corporate lawyers in the Pacific Northwest *long before* Bill invented any software. But Dad was nothing compared to Mom! Bill's mother, Mary Gates, was the granddaughter of J. W. Maxwell, the founder of Seattle's National City Bank in 1906. At the time Bill was founding what became known as Microsoft, Mary was one of America's most connected businesswomen. First, she served as a University of Washington regent. Were any of your parents university regents? I've never even *known* a regent! To be honest, I don't even know what the heck a regent does! Do you? She was also on the board of directors of First Interstate Bank and Pacific Northwest Bell. Were any of your parents on the boards of the biggest companies in your region? I've never even *known* anyone who served on a major company's board! But wait, it gets much richer (pun intended). Mary Gates also served on the national board of directors of United Way, and who do you suppose served alongside her on that same board? John Opel, CEO of IBM. Can you imagine how powerful this woman must have been to be named to the national board of one of the biggest charities in the world? She was a friend and colleague of the CEO of IBM! I don't even know the *name* of the CEO of IBM. Do you?

While serving at that board table with IBM's CEO, IBM just happened to choose Mary Gates's son, Bill, to develop the operating system (called MS-DOS) for all IBM personal computers. Now, *that's* a break you don't get every day! Have you ever gotten a break like that? But, of course, that's not the kind of break we mere mortals get. By the way, poor Bill also just happened to have had a multimillion-dollar trust, set up by his banker great-grandfather on the day he was born.

According to Microsoft legend, Bill dropped out of Harvard to create Microsoft and change the world. Do you think that maybe one of the reasons he was so quick to take that risk was that he had no worry about who would pay the bills? And poor Bill just happened to spend his early years at Lakeside School. Lakeside is *the* most prestigious and expensive private school in the Pacific Northwest. Guess who he met and befriended there? Another fellow Lucky Sperm Club member, Paul Allen, who joined him in founding Microsoft. Oh, and by the way, another

Lakeside classmate was Craig McCaw, the billionaire who sold the cellular phone licenses he obtained from the United States government to AT&T for over $11 billion. Who says fancy prep schools and Lucky Sperm Club connections don't pay off? You know what they say: It takes a billionaire to make a billionaire.

Here's an interesting little P.S. to the Bill Gates story. In case you haven't caught his act on the talk-show circuit, Bill Gates's father, Bill Gates Jr., is constantly in the news as a huge Democrat contributor who is fighting with all he's got to keep estate taxes as high as possible in the interest of "fairness." Funny, huh? Bill Gates Jr. wouldn't know the meaning of "fair" if it struck him in the face. If he wants to keep estate taxes at 50 percent or higher, it's either because (a) he feels so guilty about what he and his son have accomplished because of their fortunate birth, or (b) he and his son have so much money that it wouldn't matter if tax rates at death were 99 percent—they'd still have enough left over to buy and sell you and me a thousand times over! Estate taxes, like income taxes, are used by the superwealthy to keep the playing field *unfair*. If I have to give half of my $5 million estate to Uncle Sam, and Bill Gates has to give half of his $70 billion away, whose kids have the big advantage coming out of the funeral? Actually, it's more likely that I'll be forced to pay 50 percent tax rates at death because of Bill Gates Jr.'s lobbying, while billionaires like Gates are able to shelter 100 percent of their fortunes in offshore trusts, and along the way give their children control over companies that pay them multimillion-dollar salaries and dividends. So the next time some spoiled-brat, silver-spoon, Lucky Sperm Club, Ivy League—educated, rich kid talks about "fairness," do you and me both a favor and laugh in his face. After all, people like Bill Gates Jr. can *afford* to be Democrats. The rest of us just don't have that luxury!

Any liberal billionaire you hear talking about "fairness" and redistribution of wealth is either feeling the heavy guilt of knowing deep down that he has never earned a thing—that every job, connection, and dollar has been handed to him on a silver platter since birth, and that without all those advantages, street-smart guys like you and me would clean his clock every single time—or owes his liberal philosophy to complete hypocrisy and a desire to keep guys or gals like you and me from ever acquiring enough wealth to compete on a level playing field with them. Either way, understand that nothing they do or believe is *ever* "fair," and it is certainly *not* in your best interest.

One thing about Millionaire Republicans is that we seldom beat around the bush. You may like us or you may hate us, but we're not hypocrites. We'll tell you what we think. And I hope by now you know why Millionaire Republicans like me disagree so vehemently with liberal economic philosophy. I'm just a street kid from the Bronx borderline. I had little or no help from Daddy. No doors were opened for me. Yet today I stand before you a Millionaire Republican.

Amazingly, there are millions more just like me, and many far wealthier than me. We are self-made, self-starters who started at the bottom, asked for nothing from government, worked our butts off, and made it to the top by having the *right* attitude (the Millionaire Republican attitude). No, there aren't many of us in a league with Donald Trump, Bill Gates, Paul Allen, or Craig McCaw. But we've come an incredible distance from where we started! We faced and overcame challenges that Trump or Gates never even knew existed. We *earned* our wealth and success. We beat the million-to-one odds. Millionaire Republicans like me feel no guilt and no desperate need to give much of what we've earned away to the government in outrageous taxes. We feel no need to accept punishment for our success, or to reward those who did not work as hard, or as smartly, or as creatively, or as tenaciously as we did. No sir. We know that we've earned every cent and do not feel a moment's regret! Learning how to play the game from billionaires like Trump or Gates is a nonstarter (unless you started with their big bucks). But can you learn from a little ol' self-made millionaire like me? As one of the most successful professional gamblers in the world, I have a clear answer: *You bet you can.*

· 7 ·

Big Fat Liberal Lies

TAXES AND THE WEALTHY

A government which robs Peter to pay Paul can always depend on the support of Paul.
—GEORGE BERNARD SHAW

Before I give you the secrets to wealth and success, it's important that you understand that the Liberal Democrat's biggest lie involves taxes and the wealthy. Taxation is a controversial and emotional issue. Liberal Democrats' mantra is "Tax the rich; it's only fair." Their argument is threefold: (a) the more money you make, the higher the tax rate you should pay; (b) the rich can afford it; and (c) taxing the rich helps the poor and struggling lower classes. Well, that philosophy, and all the liberal fallacies and misconceptions behind it, couldn't be more wrong. In fact, they are just *big fat liberal lies.*

Big Fat Lie #1: Taxes are a natural part of life.

Well, not exactly. Liberals have conveniently forgotten that the American Revolution was fought over taxes and financial freedom. Or have our liberal educators found a way to delete the Boston Tea Party from our modern history books? America was founded on the premise of "no taxation without representation." As infamous Democratic campaign strategist James Carville might phrase it, "America has *always* been about the taxes, stupid!" The colonies were much less about religious freedom than they were about money. The first colonies were actually established as a business venture. Commerce and trade were the main reasons for the founding of America. Colonists made the dangerous journey from England to the New World to build better lives for their families. Today we call it the American Dream. That dream has always been based on wealth. As Calvin Coolidge said, "The business of America is business." Always has been, always will be. Colonists were entrepreneurs. Most were wild, daring, optimistic, independent-minded risk-takers who had a disdain for government. They chose to earn their livings as farmers, merchants, shopkeepers, and saloon owners. Others were independent contractors (speculators, real estate brokers and buyers, shipbuilders, home builders, traders, hunters, fishermen). And then, of course, there were the professionals (bankers, lawyers, doctors) who lived off the entrepreneurs. How risky was doing business in those early days of America? The men who made the most money were those willing to risk death to attain wealth. The earliest traders, merchants, and speculators were at the mercy of weather and nature, savage Indians, wild animals, foreign enemies, and vicious criminals (robbers along desolate roads and pirates at sea). Government help was nonexistent. It was every man for himself. As you can probably imagine, many of these original settlers of America possessed Millionaire Republican attitudes.

And just like today, it was the wealthiest and most successful who paid most of the taxes. That's why they led the revolt! The average colonist didn't care about taxes—he rarely paid any. It was the wealthy class, the businessmen, merchants, and speculators, who revolted. The masses were either against the idea of revolution or indifferent to it. Many of the poor colonists actually sympathized with the British (just as today's poor sympathize with the Democrats). The American Revolution was triggered by a steep tax on tea (hence the Boston Tea Party) and a ruling by England that investors in the colonies could no longer "speculate" on land in the Western Region. Wealthy investors (then called "speculators") like Benjamin Franklin and many of our other Founding Fathers were outraged that their ability to make money was being reined in by the British government. This outrage led to the decision to fight a war in the name of freedom from taxation without representation. The leaders of this revolution, our Founding Fathers, were the wealthiest merchants, speculators, bankers, and tradesmen in the colonies—those with the *most* to lose. But to give you an insight into their mind-set (today it would be called the mind-set of a Millionaire Republican), those with the most to lose were also the most willing to risk it all, in order to lower their taxes and increase their financial freedom. Our Founding

Fathers considered taxes, or more accurately the right to avoid unfair taxes, *that* important.

It's interesting to note that a bloody seven-year war was fought, and thousands of Americans and British died, over taxes that were *minuscule* compared to those we willingly pay today and that liberals call "fair." That's right, the American Revolution was fought over taxes, and one small category of taxes at that—what today are called "sales taxes." There was no income tax—or *any* other tax, for that matter. Income tax didn't raise its ugly head in America until the early 1900s. And as with every tax, it started out as minuscule. That's how they all start. And then they grow and multiply into today's multiple tax levies: federal income tax, state income tax, sales tax (state and local), property tax, transaction and transfer taxes (on the purchase or sale of real estate or stocks), utilities taxes (surcharges to our phone, electric, gas bills), gasoline tax, sin taxes (on things like cigarettes and liquor), Social Security tax, Medicare tax, and of course the infamous death tax (a tax on whatever we have left at our death, after already paying all the *other* taxes).

My point: Perhaps taxes are *not* so natural after all. They certainly weren't considered natural to the businessmen and entrepreneurs who founded the greatest country in the history of civilization! All these years later, nothing much has changed. The vast majority of Americans are unconcerned, indifferent, or simply numb to high taxes. Yet a consistent 15 percent of Americans call taxes one of the most important issues in American politics. Liberals point to that small minority as proof that taxes are no longer a significant issue.

Of course only 15 percent of Americans think taxes are a huge issue—*that's because those 15 percent are the ones who pay them all.* They shoulder essentially *all* the tax burden. Not coincidentally, they are also the same 15 percent of citizens who are (as Calvin Coolidge might say) conducting the business of America. They sell the stocks, real estate, mortgages, autos, and insurance. They build and develop the homes, buildings, and roads. They build the businesses and create the jobs. And they pay virtually *all* the burdensome and outrageous taxes that Liberal Democrats call "fair." As a great American businessman once said, "The 'share the wealth' movement appeals the most to those with the least to share." There is nothing fair or "natural" about high rates of taxation if you're the one paying them.

Big Fat Lie #2:
Taxes enhance the quality of life in the community.

R eally? Whose quality of life do they supposedly enhance? Who says they enhance life? Politicians? The liberal bleeding-heart media? Those who benefit from your heavy taxes— bureaucrats and government civil servants? The fact is, I don't think high taxes enhance a *damn thing.* Want proof? I lived in New York State for twenty-eight years, and then in California for thirteen. New York and California taxpayers pay some of the most onerous taxes in the country. But they're not alone. Just look at New Jersey, Massachusetts, Connecticut, Maryland, and Illinois. These unlucky taxpayers are stuck with obscene local property taxes, sales taxes, state income taxes, and even additional city taxes for those living in New York City and other cities like it.

Finally, I got smart and escaped to Las Vegas, Nevada. Nevada has been the fastest-growing state in America for eighteen consecutive years. Las Vegas has been the fastest-growing city, and Clark County has been the fastest-growing county, for those same eighteen years. Why? For one simple reason: taxes, or to be more specific, the *lack* of them. Nevada offers zero state income tax, zero business income tax, and zero inheritance tax. Las Vegas has gained a reputation as the "Monte Carlo" of America—a tax haven free from liberal do-gooders and jealous bureaucrats. Thousands flee high-tax states like New York and California and escape to Nevada. (Las Vegas alone gains 8,000 new residents a *month.*) Nevadans are living proof of the biggest lie of all—that taxpayers get something in return for high taxes. As someone who has lived in New York, California, and now Nevada, I can tell you that I am missing *nothing* in Nevada.

So please tell me what I got in return for all those years of paying substantially more out of my earnings to state and local government? There is nothing any politician, bureaucrat, or liberal do-gooder can point to that is different or missing in my life now that I live in Nevada. All those poor taxpayers in New York, California, and all the other states like them are working extra hours every day to pay more taxes—and do you know what they get? They get to have less time to enjoy life. On an income comparable to Nevadans, they get to have smaller homes, cheaper cars, smaller retirement plans, enjoy far fewer vacations, and provide less well for their families. And what do they get in return for this sacrifice? Nothing.

Are you high-tax state residents feeling sick right about now? Wait, it gets worse. I can afford a 7,000-square-foot mansion on a world-class golf course in Las Vegas because of the taxes I *don't* pay to the state of Nevada. That extra 10 percent or more of my income (and much lower property taxes) that I save literally pays my mortgage. So in effect my home is paid for by the taxes I *don't* pay to the state of Nevada.

You see, it isn't taxes that are "fair." It is taxes that make life *unfair* for residents of high-tax states. Does it seem fair that the residents of New York and California are forced to endure a lower standard of living just to pay higher taxes? Their hard-earned money is being wasted, burned, thrown down a sewer to never return. When a businessman rips off consumers, that's called fraud. When the Mafia demands "protection money" for doing nothing, that's called extortion. But when the government demands half of your money and provides little in return, that's called taxes! I guess it's all in the wording, huh?

Not only can I live a better, wealthier life because of lower taxes, my children benefit for the rest of their lives as well. Lower taxes means that I'll save more money, so my kids can afford to go to any college in America because I can afford it (Harvard, Columbia, or Stanford, instead of a cheaper state school), which could translate into a better job and bigger salary for the rest of their lives. And when I die as a Nevada resident, my kids will collect a much larger inheritance because I saved so much extra money over the years by not paying state income taxes; and of course they'll inherit much more simply because, as a Nevada resident, I pay zero state inheritance tax upon my death. Every step of the way, my life and my family's lives are improved by paying lower taxes in Nevada. So now you can clearly see the biggest lie of all—quality of life is *not* enhanced by high taxes. It is destroyed by taxes. That old adage "you get what you pay for" does not apply to taxes. Residents of high-tax states get *nothing* for all those taxes—they are simply being ripped off by government.

Now, here's a question for you to ponder. If I got nothing for all those years of paying high taxes in New York and California except a lower quality of life, what exactly do you and I get for paying high *federal* income taxes? Does it not occur to all of you reading this right now that if we paid lower federal income taxes, our quality of life would improve even more dramatically? Yet we'd be missing nothing, just as I miss nothing by living in Nevada versus New York or California. The simple fact is, taxes are not "fair" or good or natural. They destroy your quality of life every day. They prevent you from buying a bigger home or better car. They prevent you from sending your kids to private school instead of the dangerous, failing hellholes that we call public schools. They prevent you from saving for retirement—so you'll be forced to work your fingers to the bone until the day you die.

Oh, wait, they do help someone—Liberal Democrat politicians. For them, taxes are a powerful tool to keep you dependent on their handouts by making sure that you don't have enough money to own your home, start your own business, or become a member of the Investor Class. Every dollar you pay the tax man is a dollar that robs you of the life, family, and retirement of your dreams. No, high taxes *are not* fair at all. They are the enemy of the people—at least the people who work hard, create ideas, invent products, build businesses, and achieve success. And here's an eye-opener for you—*it's* our money in the first place! It doesn't belong to government bureaucrats or the IRS. It belongs to the person who earned it. *You* earned it, *you* worked long hours for it (and, if you own your own business, *you* took all the risk). Now government is taking it from you, giving you little or nothing in return, and they don't even say "Thank you!" I can think of many words for all this, but "fair" just doesn't come to mind!

Don't get me wrong, I am not a tax avoider, nor would I ever advocate that. Paying taxes is our civic duty. There are legitimate needs for government: national defense, homeland security, police and fire departments, roads, schools, and other essential services. But those needs *do not* add up to taxes of 50 percent or higher. Countries that used to be part of the communist Soviet empire now collect flat national tax rates of 13 percent. You heard me, 13 percent federal income taxes in formerly communist countries, while we pay 50 percent tax rates in capitalist America! Liberals would argue that the top income tax rate is *only* 35 percent? Well, add on sales tax, state income tax, FICA, property tax, sin taxes, transfer taxes, utility taxes, auto registration fees, and many of us now pay in the range of 50 percent or higher—and that's *outrageous.* While I've always paid what the government bureaucrats claim is my "fair share," that doesn't mean that I have to be happy about it. It doesn't mean I won't fight to reduce my tax burden with everything I've got! I fight liberal politicians and bureaucrats every day to create a better tax system. The current one does not work. It is not even remotely "fair." It punishes those who are successful, who take all the risks, who do everything right, who follow the rules of society and make something of themselves. It rewards those who don't. I vote Republican because that is the party that understands the burdens I face, that fights on behalf of successful people, and that doesn't think wealth is something to punish or redistribute. I vote Republican because that is the party that understands that by keeping taxes low on the risk-takers and wealth-creators of the world, those productive citizens will have more money to create more jobs, opportunities, and wealth for *everyone.*

Big Fat Lie #3: The rich are just selfish.
They can afford high taxes.

First of all, what is "rich"? Experts agree that most of the so-called rich in America are actually better classified as "working rich." That means they live on their income. They are not Ted Kennedy, Bill Gates (Jr. or Sr.), John Kerry, or Paris Hilton. They don't have huge trust funds or inheritances. They are entrepreneurs, merchants, small-business owners, independent contractors, and professionals (just like the original colonists). Their income fluctuates dramatically. One year they make $250,000, and suddenly, according to Democrats, they're "rich." The next year their business collapses, the economy stagnates, or the stock market slumps, and now they are struggling to make mortgage payments. Is that rich? In reality, most of the "working rich" are simply poor at a higher level. I don't hang out with the elite, trust-fund, debutante crowd. My friends are all ambitious, driven, self-made business-owners. They make good money, but they also *spend* good money. They work hard, play hard, invest hard, and spend hard. They deserve to enjoy life. They deserve to use their own hard-earned money in any way they choose. Perhaps that's the "choice" that Democrats should be fighting for! Remember, it's our money in the first place.

Achieving the American Dream is pretty simple: fight, struggle, and overcome challenges, all so that you can provide a better life for your family. Slowly, often over many years (or generations), you build that better life—defined as a bigger house (with a bigger mortgage), more furniture to fill that bigger house (more bills), a second or third car (with more auto payments), a second vacation each year (more bills), private schools to provide your kids a better education and a better life down the road (huge bills), and more options to enjoy your life (eat out more, join a country club, play golf or tennis). The American Dream costs money—big money! The more you make, the more you naturally spend. Each step up the ladder has an entry fee. But you've worked for it. It's your money. You've earned the right to spend it as you want!

So when Liberal Democrat politicians and government bureaucrats say "Tax the rich; they can afford it," they are ignoring the realities of life. This is not a socialist or communist society. Everyone is not forced to live in small apartments with no heat. Everyone is not forced to drive Yugos. Everyone is not forced to live the same lifestyle. The whole point of capitalism is that as you make more, you spend more, to enjoy more! And spending more is good for business, good for the economy, good for America. A big house, three cars, a country-club membership, and private schools don't make you rich. They often make you *poor* (at least "cash poor"). The working rich often have the same amount of money left at the end of each month as the poor or middle class: *zip.* The working rich cannot afford more taxes any more than you can. Oftentimes the working rich are just as poor—at a much higher level!

Now, I know my liberal friends in the media, government, unions, and in education will all read this and say how selfish the rich are. Perhaps they should buy one less car, or live in a smaller house, or give up golf. But once again, liberals have missed the point—*it's our money in the first place.* I know it's hard for naïve do-gooders to understand, but the reason Millionaire Republicans own instead of rent, the reason we work 24/7, the reason we love our businesses like they're our children, the reason we have passion for our careers, is that we are capitalists. Our goal is wealth. We work that hard and that long—and that creatively and passionately—because we want the best life has to offer. We want bigger houses, more expensive cars, and vacations spent at the Four Seasons and the Ritz-Carlton instead of at the Ramada Inn or Howard Johnson. We want to fly first-class and send our kids to private schools. Those are the goals and rewards for which we work. We do it all to give our family the good life, to give our kids all the things we didn't have while growing up.

Behind door number one, we have America, where entrepreneurs give 110 percent of themselves for one reason—to get rich. Behind door number two, we have France, where the workforce is heavily unionized and demands a thirty-five-hour week—result, the economy is a massive failure with high unemployment and low productivity. Behind door number three, we have communist countries like Cuba, where virtually everyone (except the liberal politicians and their cronies) lives in utter hopeless poverty and misery. Those are your choices. *What liberals call selfish is actually the best system in world history.* What they call selfish is good for everyone, including the poor and disabled. It is a fact that the top twenty-five states in America for donating to charity (per capita) are *all* Republican red states. Thank God for "selfish" capitalists whose goal is wealth. They are responsible for building the greatest country in the history of civilization!

Big Fat Lie #4:
Taxes help poor struggling immigrants.

No they don't! Let's take my personal example. My grandparents arrived in America penniless from Germany and Russia. Just like millions of other immigrants, they started out as merchants—otherwise known today as small businessmen. My grandfather Simon Reis scrimped and saved enough after many years of slaving away as a blue-collar butcher to open his own butcher store. Every day was a new struggle, a new crisis. On many occasions he did not think he'd make it. But he survived a rough start to build a successful business. His story can be multiplied by millions of immigrants. Many of the original immigrants started out as butchers, bakers, and pushcart vendors. These were low-paying jobs—but it was the only avenue available to start building a life and achieving the American Dream. Like my grandfather, these small businessmen scrimped and saved enough to buy homes, raise families, and eventually send their kids and grandkids to college—so their kids could live a better life. The key to their success in America was always (and still is) *access to capital.* Opening your own small business requires capital. Many times it takes years or even decades to save enough capital for that one shot. And when you finally get that shot, capital is once again the crucial difference between success and failure. It's a fact that most small businesses fail within the first three years—and the reason for failure virtually 100 percent of the time is a lack of sufficient capital. (Capital gives you one crucial advantage: staying power.) Billionaire Lucky Sperm Club members like Trump, Gates, the Kennedys, or Paris Hilton do not have this problem. They have all the capital they need.

Access to capital comes down to one thing: *taxes.* It's not the money a struggling immigrant earns that matters—it's the money they *keep.* Heavy taxes kill the American Dream. The more taxes you force a poor or middle-class immigrant to pay, the less likely it will be that they can ever save the capital required to start a business; the less likely they are to ever quit their job, fire their boss, give up that "safe" paycheck, and start their own business; the less likely they are to reap the benefits of the American Dream. High tax rates are not good for the poor or middle class. *High taxes are not good for anyone.* They kill your dreams, they limit your options, they lower the quality of your life (and the lives of all the generations that follow). Benjamin Franklin and our Founding Fathers had it right over two centuries ago. They believed that lower taxes, limited government interference, and more financial freedom were worth fighting for, even *dying* for! They were right then, and they are still right today.

Big Fat Lie #5: *The success and wealth of the rich do not trickle down.*

L et me tell you, I have a *great* life! I live in a mansion overlooking five lakes, seven waterfalls, snowcapped mountains, the signature fifth hole of one of most beautiful golf courses in America, and the spectacular twinkling lights of the Vegas Strip. I just bought my dream ski vacation home on the slopes of Deer Valley, Utah. I drive the best cars and eat out at the best restaurants. My children, God willing, will be able to attend any college in America, no matter the price. But I also pay a lot of taxes, and when I spend all that money on the luxuries above, I pay even more taxes (sales taxes, property taxes, payroll taxes on all the salaries I fund with my spending). Let's look at where that money goes.

My expenditures are divided into three primary categories: taxes, living expenses, and investments. While the money I pay in taxes builds infrastructure and provides government services and jobs, it has a relatively stagnant impact on the economy and the "social good." The money I spend on living expenses has a much greater impact and a multiplying effect on the economy, as what I spend here supports businesses that create jobs. Because of the competitive nature of capitalism, the companies I buy from are forced to continually provide the goods and services they sell at ever more efficient prices. (Government, of course, is just the opposite. The more inefficient government is, the more it is rewarded with ever larger budgets and bigger staffs.)

But the money I spend on investments (my home, vacation home, investment properties, stocks, businesses) provides by far the most benefit to the economy and the most social good. It has a multiplying effect that dwarfs all other kinds of spending. The money that I invest provides financing for the medical and technological breakthroughs that enhance the standard of living for us all. It provides the opportunity for entrepreneurs to have access to the capital to start and grow new businesses. And, most important, it creates the businesses and jobs of the future, making the pie bigger and bigger, so our children will have a thriving, expanding economy and their own opportunity to achieve the American Dream.

Let me give you just one specific personal example. I started my company GWIN Inc. in the year 2000. To do that I had to raise close to $20 million from investors. It costs a lot of money to build and grow a new business from scratch. My company has been no different. We have employed hundreds of people and spent tens of millions of dollars—with advertising agencies, media brokers, TV and radio networks, computer and phone companies. We've spent hundreds of thousands on insurance alone. Little old me (by starting this one business) contributed about $40 million to the American economy all by myself. What if I'd never started my company? There'd be a $40 million hole in the economy—and hundreds more Americans unemployed. At various times, many of my employees were able to buy homes because of the company I founded. Each of them hired contractors, carpenters, roofers, plumbers, electricians, landscapers. Each of them made real estate brokers, insurance agents, and home builders a little wealthier. Each of my hundreds of employees goes out to eat, to the movies, gambling in Vegas casinos, buys gas and groceries. It goes on and on. Think of the taxes—income taxes, transfer taxes, sales taxes, property taxes, payroll taxes—generated simply because I decided to start one small business! All of this without me even mentioning what I've personally spent and the income taxes I've personally paid. I've created a mini-economy—or, as I call it, "Wayne's World"—all by my lonesome. The U.S. Army ads talk about an "Army of One." I'm an "Economy of One." A money-making, money-spending consumer machine! Think of the economic impact of just one Millionaire Republican. One man (and remember, I'm no Donald Trump or Bill Gates) *can* make a difference in the American economy. So it turns out that success and wealth don't "trickle" down—*they flow like a raging river.*

Think about all of this the next time you start to think the wealth and success of Millionaire Republicans are "unfair." If we can keep taxes low (and government limited), we'll all have more money available to spend. We'll create more jobs, start more businesses, hire more employees, close more deals, buy more real estate and stocks, fill those houses with more furniture and art. We'll give more to charity. And with all of this, we'll willingly and cheerfully create more taxes at all levels. So why do Liberal Democrats want to take away more of my money and give it to an already bloated, inefficient government bureaucracy, or redistribute it to those less productive members of society? Shouldn't the goal be to leave as much money in the hands of the biggest producers and job creators? Shouldn't the goal be to lift more average Americans up, instead of pushing successful ones down? Shouldn't we be trying to create more millionaires instead of more government programs and more Americans dependent on them? Oh silly me, I guess I forgot—that would create more Republican voters and contributors, wouldn't it? Liberal politicians and bureaucrats could not allow that, could they?

A Closing Thought on Taxes

I'd like to give you "food for thought" about the lunacy and idiocy of the current tax system, as set up by liberal bureaucrats with no understanding of capitalism. Suppose I went to dinner once a month for twenty years with my old college classmates. And suppose because I'm the richest and most successful, the other nineteen "friends" demand I pay the entire bill every time. The bill is $1,000. I am forced to pay it twelve times a year for twenty years because "Wayne is rich. He can afford it." Would that be fair to me? After twenty years of carrying the freight for all nineteen friends, I could wind up the poorest! Somehow I don't think that's the definition of "fair." But wait—it gets better!

Suppose the restaurant announced that because I've been such a good customer for twenty years, they've decided to give me a 20 percent discount, so now I'll pay "only" $800 every month. That sounds good to me, but my liberal college classmates say it's "unfair." They're angry that I'm the rich one, and they think I don't deserve a break. In fact, they think *they* deserve the 20 percent refund. After all, they're not as successful as me—they need the money more than I do. So their definition of "fair" is that I continue to pay a $1,000 bill each time we meet, they get their meal for free, and then they split the $200 refund among themselves. The result is that they'll each earn about $10 profit every time they eat with me. The gall! The audacity! Who'd ever agree to that deal? Only an idiot, right?

Well, that is *exactly* what's happening to high earners in the American income tax system every day. Those deemed wealthy pay virtually all the taxes, thereby being punished for their success. When the government finally decides to give a tax break to the highest income earners because we pay most of the taxes (and take all the risk, and create all the jobs), Liberal Democrats immediately scream in anger and outrage, insisting that any refund should rightfully go to the poorest Americans. Otherwise, they protest, "it's a *giveaway* to the rich." They demand that the tax cut go to anyone and everyone but me. First of all, how can it be called a "giveaway" to simply allow me to keep a little more of my own money? It can't be unfair to give someone back a small portion of their own money, can it? And secondly, if you do agree to cut taxes, shouldn't it rightfully go to those who actually wrote the checks and paid the taxes? Liberals actually try to paint it as "fair" to give back my tax money to someone else who never paid *any* in the first place! That's logic only a lawyer could understand.

Do you know what I'd call that? A *mugging!* Now, here's how my college classmates story ends: When the nineteen classmates, who have never paid a single bill, demanded the 20 percent refund, their rich classmate balked. "Enough is enough," I said. I put my foot down and explained that it's my money in the first place, and therefore the refund is rightfully mine. The nineteen classmates promptly beat up their good friend. They kicked me, punched me, spit on me, and left me bleeding and unconscious in an alley. A month later, the classmates showed up for dinner as usual, but guess who was missing? That's right, their rich friend finally got the message and took his marbles to play elsewhere. None of the nineteen minded. To the contrary, they laughed about the butt-kicking they gave the rich guy. They taunted their old buddy. They said in unison, "Good riddance to Root." Then the bill came. Panic set in. "But who's going to pay the bill?" they suddenly cried in unison. That night those nineteen friends washed dishes in the back of the restaurant. They never came back. Their free dinners were over forever.

That, my friends, is what Millionaire Republicans call a happy ending! Keep attempting to take more and more of our hard-earned money; keep using our hard-earned money to create more government programs, so that there is a never-ending demand for more taxes; keep calling a refund of a small portion of our own money an "unfair giveaway"; keep insisting that the "fair" thing to do is give the refund of our money to others who never paid a dime in the first place; and I promise you that one day we will decide to never show up at the dinner table again. Then the free lunches and dinners will be over forever. Then the question will become, who exactly will pay for America's bills?

My prediction: An awful lot of people are going to be left cleaning dishes in the back of the restaurant, for an awful long time!

· 8 ·

The Red Storm Revolution

THRIVING IN A
REPUBLICAN RED WORLD

The future of America is bright red.

—WAYNE ALLYN ROOT

A s we come to the "meat" of this book—the 18 Republican Secrets you'll need to succeed and thrive—I want to first explain why it is so important for you to think like a Millionaire Republican. I make predictions for a living, and I'm so good at it that my talents as a soothsayer have made me millions of dollars. I've made my predictions on TV networks like CNBC, ABC, USA, Spike, FOX SportsNet, FOX News Channel, and CNN. (And this year you can find me Saturday mornings during the football season on Superstation WGN.) Thousands of private clients pay millions of dollars annually for my sports predictions. On the political side, only days before the 2004 election, I predicted (on CNBC) that George W. Bush would win by three points and thirty or more electoral votes. To my knowledge, that was the most accurate prediction of any political pundit or pollster in America (and it came at the moment that most pollsters thought John Kerry was pulling ahead). I tell you all this because I now think it is important that you heed my biggest prediction of all: A Red Storm is upon us. All of you must start thinking, acting, and investing like Millionaire Republicans to capitalize on the historic political realignment now occurring. You know that famous saying, "When in Rome, do as the Romans do"? Well, in my opinion, Rome has just gone Republican, and you can no longer *afford* to think like a Liberal Democrat.

Currently, the GOP controls the United States presidency, the House of Representatives, the Senate, the Supreme Court, and a majority of governorships and state legislatures across America. That is not a fluke. *This Republican dominance at all levels of government will not only continue—it will increase.* I believe that the GOP is entering a phase of dominance similar to that of FDR and the Democrats in 1932. The GOP will dominate all levels of government for many years to come. One of my goals with this book is to empower readers to plan, profit, and capitalize in the midst of this "Red Storm."

Where you choose to live, how you choose to think, and what type of investments you make will all determine whether you will survive or thrive in the twenty-first century. As I explained earlier in Chapter Two, "The Divided States of America," we are fast becoming a country of two peoples. Americans are moving to red states in droves. These are states where government is smaller, taxes are lower, jobs are plentiful, churches abound, and small businesses are thriving. Blue states will continue to lose population, power, funding from government, electoral votes, and political prominence. What will be left are two Americas: red states full of young, healthy, daring entrepreneurial risk-takers with high incomes, advanced levels of education, healthy levels of marriage and church attendance, and robust levels of business creation and economic growth, and on the opposite end of the spectrum, blue states—best described as aging, poverty-stricken, drug-addicted, violent crime–infested regions with decaying infrastructures, overflowing welfare rolls, and residents who are too fearful to start a business, who are dependent on government, and who continue to demand ever more services, even as they're stuck with ever-higher taxes and regulations. Those blue states and the people stuck in them are destined for tough times. Your success therefore depends on:

- facing these facts—no matter your political orientation.
- understanding the new reality of the two Americas.
- knowing how to react to this dramatic change, and capitalizing on it.
- *investing* in this new dynamic.

First of all, is this fact or just my opinion? Will the GOP really continue to dominate at all levels of government and become the long-term majority party, or is this just a temporary status? Liberal Democrat leaders and so-called experts from liberal academia and the liberal news media will, of course, tell

you that this Republican dominance is not only temporary—
but that it is not even dominance in the first place. They will
point to President Bush's three-point victory margin as proof
that Republican dominance is a mirage. But let's look at a few
facts that point to the dramatic Republican Red Storm that is
gathering.

GEORGE W. BUSH RECEIVED THE MOST
VOTES OF ANY PRESIDENTIAL CANDIDATE
IN THE HISTORY OF AMERICA.

Democrats have been in decline (on the presidential level) since
1964. Jimmy Carter and Bill Clinton are the only Democrats to
win the presidency in those forty years. Both were exceptions
to the rule. They were moderate Southern Democrats, who
campaigned almost as conservatives. And in case you didn't notice the circumstances of their victories, let me point them out:
Carter won a close victory in the immediate aftermath of Wa-
tergate—the worst scandal in American political history. And
Clinton was the most charismatic politician of his generation—gifted with good looks, great charm, and one-of-a-kind
oratory skills. Clinton also had the luxury of popular independent candidate H. Ross Perot on the ballot in both of his elections. Take away those extraordinary circumstances and no
Democrat has won the White House "fair and square" in almost
half a century. I'd call that a strong sign of a Red Storm! And

I've got a news flash for Democrats: It's just going to keep getting worse!

BUSH'S THREE-PERCENTAGE-POINT
VICTORY WAS ACTUALLY A LARGER
PERCENTAGE OF THE VOTE THAN
ANY DEMOCRAT PRESIDENTIAL
CANDIDATE HAS RECEIVED SINCE
LYNDON JOHNSON IN 1964.

That's right, boys and girls. Perhaps your history teachers forgot to mention that Bill Clinton, the man universally declared "a popular president" by the media, *never* won a majority of the American vote. Once again, liberal media bias shows up. Clinton was lauded again and again for his "popularity," yet he received lower vote totals and lower percentages of the electorate than George W. Bush in 2004. But it's not just Clinton—no Democrat has managed to win the presidency by as large a margin as "W" since 1964.

PRESIDENT BUSH BECAME THE FIRST
UNITED STATES PRESIDENT SINCE FDR IN
1936 TO WIN REELECTION WHILE HIS PARTY
GAINED SEATS IN BOTH THE SENATE AND
THE HOUSE OF REPRESENTATIVES.

The GOP has more congressmen than they've had at any time since 1946—and more senators than at any time since 1931. Adding to the GOP domination, Republicans also increased their majority of governorships. And they held their majority of state legislators after half a century in the minority. All of this is just more proof of an FDR-like Republican realignment in progress.

IN 2004, PRESIDENT BUSH AND THE
REPUBLICAN PARTY WON 81 PERCENT OF
THE COUNTIES IN AMERICA!

(To be exact, "W" won 2,533 counties). Yes, you heard right, I said 81 percent! America's map is completely dominated by Republican red, and this pattern isn't going to change anytime soon. A recent cover story in *USA Today* reported that not only are nine of the ten fastest-growing states Republican red states, but nine out of the ten fastest-growing counties in America from 2000 to 2004 were in Republican red states! But this dominant red pattern even shows up in liberal states like California and New York, providing more proof of two very divided Americas. In both New York and California, red counties dominate, and most of them are affluent suburban and exurban areas. The few blue counties (dominated by the Democratic Party) are, for the most part, poverty-stricken inner cities or lower middle-class blue-collar union strongholds.

If your goal is to participate in the new ownership society, to *own* versus rent your future, you have a distinct choice. You can go back to the past with the party of FDR and spend your life surrounded by renters, protesters, complainers, and people dependent on government help just to survive. Or you can move forward to the future and join the thriving ownership class that lives, works, and plays in prosperous, thriving, low-tax red counties and states. That's the Republican version of "choice"!

PRESIDENT BUSH PROVED THAT THE 2000 ELECTION WAS NOT A FLUKE BY INCREASING HIS VOTE SHARE IN FORTY-EIGHT OUT OF FIFTY STATES AND IN 87 PERCENT OF THE COUNTIES IN AMERICA!

Now, those are eye-opening numbers! But what makes those results even worse for Democrats is my belief that "W" was actually a flawed candidate. First of all, Bush is certainly not a great orator. Most experts will tell you he lost all three presidential debates with John Kerry. Second, he presided over a lousy economy and falling stock market—usually a sure sign that the incumbent president will be thrown out of office. Third, his first term was dominated by the controversial and unpopular Iraq war and massive antiwar and anti-Bush protests across the globe. Fourth, everything that could possibly go wrong during his campaign *did*—from lousy economic and job figures to the ever-increasing death toll of U.S. soldiers in Iraq to the death of Christopher Reeve (reminding voters of Bush's unpopular stance against stem-cell research) to the dramatic rise in the price of oil. Fifth, pragmatic candidates of both parties historically head for the political middle ground, trying to appeal to moderate voters—but not Bush. With "W," what you see is what you get! Bush played the part of conservative Christian, which he is, throughout the entire campaign. And because of this he gave the liberal media a great opportunity to paint him and the GOP as extreme, radical, and out of touch with mainstream America. Despite all of that, Bush received more votes than any presidential candidate in history, and the GOP won 81 percent of all the counties in America! Amazing. "W" may actually have been the worst candidate the GOP could have run! His clear-cut victory bodes well for GOP dominance for many years to come.

PERHAPS MOST IMPORTANT OF ALL, THE
2004 PRESIDENTIAL ELECTION INVOLVED
THE BIGGEST TURNOUT OF ANY
PRESIDENTIAL ELECTION SINCE 1968.

For years we've all heard that to win, the GOP needs low voter turnout. The theory has gone "Republicans pray for rain on election day." Well, that theory was put to rest and buried in 2004. The most voters in almost forty years turned out at the polls, and they voted Republican across the board (for president, senator, congressman, governor, and state legislator)!

BUSH AND THE REPUBLICAN PARTY
DRAMATICALLY IMPROVED THEIR
PERCENTAGE OF THE VOTE IN CATEGORIES
ACROSS THE POLITICAL SPECTRUM.

The GOP's share of the Jewish vote increased from 16 percent in 1996 to 25 percent in 2004. Their share of the Latino vote increased from 21 percent to 44 percent. Their share of the Catholic vote increased from 37 percent to 52 percent. Their share of union votes increased from 30 percent to 40 percent. Their share of female votes increased from 38 percent to 48 percent. Their share of suburban votes increased from 42 percent to 52 percent. Their share of the exurban vote (areas just beyond suburbs) increased from 47 percent to 59 percent. These results show the difficult job that faces future Democratic candidates.

The GOP's share of their own base also increased dramatically.

The GOP's share of conservative votes increased from 71 percent in 1996 to 84 percent in 2004. And while the percentage of voters declaring themselves "Evangelical Christians" increased from 14 percent to 23 percent of the total American electorate, those same 27.4 million Evangelicals voted 78 percent Republican in 2004. This base of Conservative Christians will help to ensure a red Republican future for many years to come.

The demographics and economics of America do not support the Democrats.

Think back to the chapter on the Divided States of America. Three groups that dominate the *finances* of America support the GOP: home owners, stockholders, and small-business owners. They make up the crucial Investor Class. All three groups are ascending. For the first time ever, home ownership levels are fast approaching 70 percent. *A majority of home owners vote Republican.*

Owning stocks is no longer for the wealthy alone. Because of the success of IRAs, SEP IRAs, Keogh accounts, and 401(k)s, more Americans own stocks than ever before. *A majority of stock-holders vote Republican.*

And this is the generation of small-business owners, sole proprietors, and independent contractors. *An overwhelming major-ity of small-business owners votes and supports the GOP.* The GOP utilized almost 90,000 small-business leaders in 2004 to preach the GOP pro-business agenda across the country. As the ranks of the Investor Class continue to grow, the Republican Party will dominate political fund-raising as never before!

The GOP has the advantage with young voters.

George W. Bush is no dummy. "W" is pushing the privatization of Social Security for two very good reasons: First is the obvious—it's an economically sound way to increase dwindling future Social Security benefits through the magic of compounding (higher interest rates from higher stock returns). But second is the not-so-obvious reason—it is a truly brilliant *political* strategy. Yes, the odds are against privatization—there may simply be too many liberal special interests aligned against it (even though the most attractive pension plans in all of America belong to liberal bureaucrats—state and federal employees who already invest in a private stock program almost identical to what privatization would look like). But even if the idea of privatization fails due to ignorance and deceit, Bush has accomplished something crucial to help ensure a half century of GOP dominance. He has convinced America's younger generation that the GOP is the party of solutions and creative ideas. By attempting to educate and empower younger voters on the problems of Social Security and the benefits of privatization, "W" has moved an entire generation to the *right*. The older voters who are fighting change might have won a short-term battle, but "W" and the GOP have won the more important war for the hearts, minds, and votes of the next generation.

The GOP has an electoral edge.

A majority of young and financially well-off voters (home owners, stockholders, small-business owners) are moving in droves to red states. These states are all in the West and South, led by Nevada, the fastest-growing state for the eighteenth consecutive year. Ten people an *hour* are moving to Las Vegas alone! The result is that these fast-growing red states are adding political clout by the hour! You can count on Republican red states adding congressional seats and electoral votes in the coming years. The result is that it is getting harder and harder for the Democratic Party to cobble together enough electoral votes to win a presidential election—and almost impossible for them to win back Congress. Do the math—the numbers are all going against Democrats.

How dominant is the GOP control over red states? In the 2004 presidential election, eight Republican red states in the Rocky

Mountain West handed Bush and the GOP a 44–0 electoral victory! Those states are all gaining electoral votes. A recent article in the *Los Angeles Times* indicates that the Democrats are targeting those same eight red states for future elections, simply because the South is so dominant for the GOP that those eight states look *competitive* by comparison. Can you even imagine how bad things have gotten for the Democratic strategists? Hey, you may not get this info from the liberal media or hear it at Hollywood parties, but it's fast becoming a red world out there!

THE GOP WILL DOMINATE PRESIDENTIAL
POLITICS FOR YEARS TO COME BECAUSE OF
A HUGE EDGE IN THE QUALITY OF
ELECTABLE CANDIDATES.

The GOP has an almost endless supply of attractive presidential candidates: **John McCain**— a true American hero, politically moderate, with star power and crossover voter appeal that could result in a GOP landslide in 2008. **Rudolph Giuliani**— another moderate political star with strong crossover appeal; but Rudy has an even bigger ace in the hole: He can win New York, which all but guarantees a GOP presidential victory. **Jeb Bush**—a popular Southern governor, Bush carries on the dynasty name in American politics, with the bonus of guaranteeing a GOP presidential victory in America's third most populous state (Florida). Secretary of State **Condoleezza Rice**—a great

American success story, combined with a popular appeal to both minorities and female voters that could diversify the GOP base and offset any Hillary Clinton advantage (I see Condoleezza as the next GOP vice president). **Mitt Romney**—movie-star handsome and a moderate GOP governor who has proven he can balance a budget (the Salt Lake Olympic Games) and win in the most liberal state in America; if Mitt can win in Massachusetts, he could sweep America in a landslide. Virginia Senator **George Allen**—the charismatic son of a true American football legend and the popular senator of a populous red state. **George Pataki**—the three-term GOP governor of New York; **Bill Frist**—senate majority leader. The GOP's "back bench" includes stars like **Elizabeth Dole** (North Carolina senator and wife of former GOP presidential candidate Bob Dole); **Newt Gingrich** (former Speaker of the House); and, of course, "The Governator," **Arnold Schwarzenegger** (yes, we must first pass a constitutional amendment to allow foreigners to become president after twenty years of citizenship, but Arnold has been known to make miracles happen; we may yet see President Arnold by 2012 or 2016).

Now let's look at the list of Democratic presidential candidates. They are all *flawed.* First and foremost, at the top of the list is Senator **Hillary Clinton.** The left wing of the Democratic party actually thinks she'd make a "dream candidate." They are so out of touch that they don't realize she is actually a *nightmare!* Mrs. Clinton has a liberal voting record that will make her one of the great political targets of all time. She is a controversial lightning rod equal to or worse than Newt Gingrich, her equivalent on the GOP side. Did you notice I didn't even include Newt in my serious list of GOP presidential possibilities? The GOP list is so deep and attractive, Newt is far toward the bottom. The Democrats are in deep trouble when their most controversial candidate is is at the top of their list! Hillary is a Northeast intellectual, feminist liberal who will always be remembered as the woman who tried to stuff socialized medicine down America's throat. Famous or not, beloved by female liberals or not, she could be the most *unelectable* Democrat since George McGovern (whose presidential campaign she once worked on).

Senator John Kerry certainly remains near the top of any Democrat list for 2008. But once again, he is seriously flawed and serves as proof that Democrats never learn their lesson. And what is that lesson? Simple: Only a *moderate* Southern Democrat has a shot at the presidency. As I pointed out earlier, in almost forty years the only Democrats elected to the White House have been Jimmy Carter and Bill Clinton. Liberals, especially those from the Northeast, have always been dead on arrival—think Ted Kennedy, Michael Dukakis, John Kerry, Edmund Muskie, Hubert Humphrey, and George McGovern. Kerry could make history by joining that list for a second time!

Now the Democrats and their loyal media lackeys are anointing **Barack Obama,** my Columbia college classmate, as the next savior for the Democratic Party. I like Barack. He is an electrifying speaker. He has a terrific story and a mixed-race family history that fits perfectly into popular twenty-first-century American culture. He appears to be a nice guy, too. But Barack is out of the mainstream—his voting record is so far to the left, it leans to socialist! To top it off, the only thing Americans despise more than career politicians is intellectual, book-smart Ivy League lawyers who have accomplished nothing in the real world. Obama has spent his entire adult life as an Ivy League student (Columbia, Harvard), lawyer, and politician. He's never earned a dime in the real world, never started a business, never made a payroll. Would you put the most powerful economy in world history in the hands of someone with those credentials?

Is America ready for a black president? Absolutely! Colin Powell or Condoleezza Rice could be elected tomorrow. But America is not ready for a *liberal* black president. Obama has the same liberal extremist views as Jesse Jackson and Al Sharpton. He only recently repackaged them to sound moderate. Unless he changes his voting record radically over the coming years as a U.S. senator, his chance of being elected president is slim.

Next we come to **John Edwards,** the 2004 Democratic Party vice presidential candidate. Edwards is handsome, charismatic, and a Southerner. Many Democrats will say he is the perfect candidate—an updated version of Bill Clinton. How we deceive ourselves! Clinton sounded like a moderate, had a voting record to match, and literally campaigned as a conservative.

(Oh, if only he'd governed that way!) And, most important, although he was a lawyer, Clinton never practiced as a lawyer. If there's any symbol of liberalism that is hated more by Americans than a Northeast intellectual liberal, it's a personal-injury lawyer. Edwards wears a big fat target on his chest! He is the quintessential ambulance chaser and class-action fat cat trial lawyer rolled into one. He has gotten rich by targeting doctors and hospitals, the worst kind of vile lawyer despised by Americans. All his Southern advantages are nullified by his choice of profession and a voting record as a U.S. senator that is among the most liberal and (of course) pro–trial lawyer in American politics. Edwards is "fatally" flawed.

Finally, we save the "best" for last: **Al Gore.** Here's another Southern Democrat who not only reminds supporters of Clinton but even served alongside Bubba. The problem is that Gore is Clinton *without* the personality—actually without *any* personality! He's Gore the Bore. The old joke actually fits. The Secret Service tags each president and VP with nicknames like "Warrior," "Cowboy," or "Giant." The joke goes that Al Gore is so boring, his nickname is "Al Gore"! I don't see America reaching back into its past to elect Al Gore. A presidential candidate must have some personality. Gore the Bore is simply stiff as a board. (And a bit loony as well—did you see that Grizzly Adams beard after he lost in 2000?)

HILLARY, KERRY, OBAMA, EDWARDS, AND GORE ARE THE LEADING DEMOCRATIC CANDIDATES FOR THE FORESEEABLE FUTURE, AND *ALL* ARE EXTREME LIBERALS WITH VOTING RECORDS THAT WILL HANG LIKE AN ALBATROSS AROUND THEIR NECKS!

They are all flawed choices, yet they are the best the Democrats have to offer. Giuliani, McCain, Romney, Rice, or Jeb Bush can all eat the top Democratic choices for breakfast. Unless the field of candidates changes radically and a moderate, strong-on-defense, Southern Democrat appears out of the blue (Mark Warner of Virginia, for example), I predict GOP control of the White House for many years to come.

So there you have it. This professional prognosticator believes that the GOP will dominate American politics (on all levels) for the foreseeable future. We are seeing an historic realignment that resembles what the Democrats created in 1932 under FDR.

In the next chapter of this book, you'll learn the 18 Republican Secrets of Mega-Wealth and Unlimited Success that will give you the tools and insights to capitalize and profit in the midst of this Red Storm!

· 9 ·

The 18 Republican Secrets
of Mega-Wealth and
Unlimited Success!

Millionaire Republicans aren't born. They are self-made.

—WAYNE ALLYN ROOT

Now it is time to teach you the secrets that will make you wealthy and successful beyond your wildest dreams. By now, it should be no secret that your most important goal should be *ownership*. Own—don't rent—your home, your career, your retirement, your financial future, your *life*. This chapter is quite simply an instruction manual for how to *own* your life. No matter where you are starting from, no matter your age (later in this chapter, you'll hear that Americans over the age of fifty are starting and owning businesses like never before), no matter your current income, if you follow my secrets for investing and thriving in a Republican Red Storm, you have a great shot at joining me as a Millionaire Republican and owning the life of your dreams. That's what this book is all about—*ownership*. Let's get started!

Secret #1: Own Your Destiny—Go West (or South), Young Man

If you think like a Millionaire Republican you can succeed no matter where you live and work. But that doesn't mean that you shouldn't try to increase your odds of success by moving to where opportunity is the greatest. When the infamous bank robber Willie Sutton was asked why he robbed banks, he answered, "Because that's where the money is!" Sometimes life is just that simple! My advice: Go where the money is. Improve your chances of success by relocating to where there is more opportunity. By now, I hope you'll agree that we are in the midst of a Republican Red Storm. The kind of Americans who own (whether it be stocks, homes, businesses, or investment property) are moving to red states. It is important to surround yourself with people like that, to live where they live. Why? It doesn't take a brain surgeon or Harvard MBA to realize that your odds of success are significantly improved in a hot market. More buyers with disposable income means more opportunities and faster appreciation of real estate. More prosperous people moving into your geographic area creates more opportunities to capitalize. It is a positive and prosperous cycle (a red Republican cycle). It's not that you can't make money or build a prosperous business in New York, Boston, or Los Angeles—of course you can. But your odds of doing it—and doing it *faster*—

increase dramatically in places where the population and opportunities are growing the fastest.

While more opportunity is the number-one reason to move to fast-growing red states, lower taxes and less government interference are close seconds. The fact is, you can open a business much more quickly and for far less money in places like Las Vegas, Nevada, Nashville, Tennessee, or Austin, Texas, than you can in New York, Chicago, or Los Angeles. So, while that dream of yours to open a restaurant, anti-aging center, beauty salon, or auto repair shop may be impossible in New York, it's a reality in Austin, Boise, Salt Lake City, Las Vegas, or Scottsdale. But it gets even better. Perhaps the biggest advantage of all is that once you earn money in red states, you'll get to *keep* more of it (because of lower state income taxes). And keeping more of your own money allows you to reinvest that extra money in even more real estate, stocks, and small businesses. So my very first secret for aspiring Millionaire Republicans is to move to where taxes are low, regulations are few, government is small, and opportunity is as *big* as the Rocky Mountains!

Where are these low-tax red states, filled with opportunity and prosperity? They are all in the West and the South. The Red Storm is strongest in states like Nevada, Arizona, Colorado, Utah, Montana, New Mexico, Idaho, Washington, Texas, Florida, Georgia, Arkansas, Tennessee, Virginia, North Carolina, and South Carolina. It is interesting to note that *all* of these "hot tickets" are low-tax states. *All* (except Washington) are dominant Republican red states. And *all* are states whose economies are *thriving*. Want more proof? Since 1990, the nine states without state income taxes have enjoyed 2.5 times the population growth and *double* the job growth of the highest income-tax states (all blue states). The regions that are struggling economically under the burden of crushing taxes are all loyal Democratic blue states. There is no coincidence here. Americans who think like Millionaire Republicans are moving out of blue states and escaping to red states.

The latest census figures report that nine of the top ten fastest-growing states (as well as sixteen of the top twenty fastest-growing) are Republican red states! From 1990 to 2003, the growth rate of small Western towns (populations of 2,500 or smaller) was *four times* the national average. And the most recent census figures show that the biggest population explosion of all is happening in the exurbs—counties on the farthest edges of metropolitan areas. Of the ten fastest-growing counties in America between 2000 and 2004, nine are located in red states! The U.S. Census Bureau just predicted that the next quarter century will be more of the same: The five states most likely to grow the fastest in the next twenty-five years— Nevada, Arizona, Utah, Florida, and Texas—are all red states! The people relocating to these Republican states are *thrivers*— high earners with lots of marketable skills, who bring with them big bank accounts, lots of disposable income, businesses, jobs, and a can-do spirit. In other words, they are *owners*—and their buying spree will take place in the red states they are moving to. The people staying put in blue states lack the education, resources, skills, savings, or know-how to relocate. The result is that these Republican red states represent the fastest-growing populations, fastest-growing economies, best business opportunities, and the best real estate opportunities. These are the states that will *thrive* in the twenty-first century, while high-tax blue states will be lucky to just survive.

Yes, it is true that if you're smart, you can succeed anywhere. But the odds of your success are certainly far higher in one of these red states.

The Pacific Research Institute rated over 100 factors to create the "U.S. Economic Freedom Index: 2004." The factors included taxes, and regulatory and fiscal burdens placed on each state's residents. Not surprisingly, the best states for economic freedom and the fastest-growing states are an almost identical match. And, not surprisingly, they are almost all red states! How dominant are Republican red states on this list? Twenty-four of the top twenty-six states voted for Bush in 2004! CNN/*Money* recently published a list of big-city tax burdens for a typical American family. The results were almost identical to the "Economic Freedom" list: twenty-one of the twenty-five lowest-tax big cities were located in Republican red states! Are you getting the picture? Republican values, principles, and habits lead to low taxes and economic freedom, which in turn lead to opportunity, job creation, economic growth, and your personal success!

On the opposite end of the spectrum are the worst-performing states—the ones with the *least* economic freedom. They are

New York (blue), California (blue), Connecticut (blue), Rhode Island (blue), Illinois (blue), Pennsylvania (blue), Minnesota (blue), Ohio (red, but just barely), New Jersey (blue), and Massachusetts (blue). All of this is just more proof that Republican thinking equals financial success and Liberal Democratic thinking equals financial distress and economic failure!

In addition to the economic reasons mentioned above, you'll also want to move to red states because they are gaining political clout. Experts predict that new congressional seats and electoral votes will be added soon in red states like Nevada, Arizona, Utah, Idaho, Florida, and Texas. This will add political power to the Republican Party, enhancing the chance for the GOP to control Congress and the presidency for decades to come. I realize many of you don't lie awake at night thinking about the importance of political power. But let me assure you, the political power of your state (or lack of it) is critical to your economic well-being. Red state residents will have political clout, which means *economic* clout and economic freedom. These politically powerful red states will gain more federal money and funding—which in turn will attract more smart, ambitious, aspiring Millionaire Republicans to move there, thereby creating more wealth and opportunity for all. And the more wealth that is created in a state, the less likely taxes will have to be raised to pay for new programs (hence, the result is your economic freedom). So my very first Millionaire Republican secret is to live in a red state and put the power of this positive and prosperous red cycle of opportunity and riches to work for you!

As a quick aside, I have a friend who works as a financial planner, who just left California to live in Las Vegas. Why did she make the move? Because over the next twenty years her tax savings from living in Nevada rather than California will pay her mortgage—she'll get a free million-dollar home! Her advice to every single one of her clients: Get out of California fast! More proof that where you live can make all the difference in the world. At least all the difference in a *red* world! My advice: Go west or south, young man (or woman)—and do it quickly.

Secret # 2: Own Republican Red Real Estate

Owning a piece of America has always been the American Dream. And owning your own home has always been smart advice. The saying "Own, don't rent" has been around for a long, long time. Obviously it is good advice, and Americans are following it in record numbers! But you don't want to own just *any* home in *any* location. You want to follow Republican Secret #1 and buy real estate *only* in red states, where growing demand means greater appreciation. As an example, let's look at my favorite town: Las Vegas, Nevada. Vegas recently became the first metropolitan area in the history of America to see residential property appreciate over 50 percent in one quarter, and over

40 percent for one full year! Is that kind of appreciation and profit really hard to understand? No! With almost 100,000 Americans escaping to Las Vegas annually from high-tax blue states, it's easy to see that demand trumps supply in Las Vegas (and will continue to do so for many years to come). The state of Nevada and the city of Las Vegas have each been number-one in America in growth for eighteen consecutive years! This mass exodus from blue states will continue unabated, far into this century—which makes owning a home in Las Vegas, Reno, Scottsdale, Tucson, Boise, Salt Lake City, Colorado Springs, Bozeman (Montana), Santa Fe, Austin, Dallas, Houston, San Antonio, Atlanta, Nashville, Little Rock, Bentonville (Arkansas), Charleston, Charlotte, Palm Beach, or Boca Raton all much better investments than owning a home in any high-tax, blue-state metropolitan area.

Are there exceptions to this rule? Of course. California cities like Brentwood, Beverly Hills, Santa Monica, Malibu, Santa Barbara, La Jolla, Palo Alto, and San Francisco may be liberal bastions, but homes have been appreciating pretty darn fast there, too. However, they started pretty high! If you already own a home in Malibu or Beverly Hills, you must already be a millionaire (just in house value alone). But if you're a young, hungry, ambitious, *aspiring* Millionaire Republican, your best bet is simple common sense: You are better off buying twice the home at half the cost in a fast-growing red state. And because those red states have lower or no state income tax, you'll be able to more quickly save the money you need for the down payment (or a second home). Pretty neat trick, huh? It's not "black magic"—it's *red* magic. I already told you the story of my friend who is getting a million-dollar home for *free* because of tax savings. Come to Las Vegas and get one for yourself. It's not a gamble—*it's a sure thing.*

In the introduction I told you that I am a fan of the best-selling book *Rich Dad, Poor Dad* and agreed with most of author Robert Kiyosaki's advice. But no one is perfect, and one thing I believe he was wrong about is home ownership. Kiyosaki recommends owning income properties (rentals) over your principal residence. He considers your home to be a money burner, as opposed to an asset. But he's dead wrong! In arriving at this conclusion he missed two key points. First, financial success (as any Millionaire Republican knows) is not about what you make, it's about what you *keep.* Your home is, by far, the single best and biggest tax deduction available. The mortgage deduction, property tax deduction, and, if you work at home (which so many Millionaire Republicans do), home office deduction, are all fantastic legal ways to lower your tax bill. Secondly, the $500,000 tax exemption for married home owners (or $250,000 for singles) is by far the greatest tax deduction in U.S. history. Every American family is allowed to sell his or her principal residence every two years and keep up to a half million dollars of profit *tax free.* That tax law alone makes owning your own home one of your best possible investments. But the bonus is *you get to live in the house while it reduces your taxes.* And Kiyosaki thinks that's a bad deal? You have to live somewhere. You might as well go for the biggest, most expensive mortgage you can afford, deduct all the interest off your tax return (up to a maximum of $1,000,000), and earn a healthy appreciation (in a red state, of course) with the bonus of up to $500,000 every two years *tax free*. On the other hand, you can't live inside your IBM or Microsoft stock—or inside your small business, your gold stockpile, or your art collection. Those may all be good investments, yet none of them provide shelter for your family. None of them provide a good night's sleep or a refreshing morning swim. None of them are tax deductible. And none of them provide tax-free profits of up to $500,000 every two years! Sorry Mr. "Rich Dad," but home ownership is the best deal in all of America!

As far as thinking (and living) like a smart Millionaire Republican, Kiyosaki loses brownie points here, too. He tells his readers that they must be frugal—I call it *stingy*. He wants you to save, save, save. He'd recommend you buy the cheapest house possible, so that you keep your expenses to a minimum. In Kiyosaki's way of thinking, all monies should be going toward your investments—things that produce positive cash flow (primarily rental properties). In most cases, he's right. But not when it comes to your principal residence. As a self-made millionaire who has made most of my money in real estate (not commercial real estate or raw land, but on the homes I've lived in), my advice is to buy *big*. Stretch beyond where you feel comfortable. Buy the biggest and best home in the best neighborhood. Just be sure you buy in "hot" growth markets (red states). And one more specific piece of advice: Americans crave security like never before. Homes in guard-gated communities are the best investment of all. They will appreciate far faster than any other location. Will the value of your home always go up? Of course not. I've owned homes for twenty years now and I've seen real estate go up and down (sometimes dramatically). But that's over the short term. As I write this, this country may actually be on the precipice of a real estate downturn. But that too shall pass. Short term you could have *paper* losses (although still living comfortably in your own home the whole time). But long term (five years or longer) in the *right* neighborhood, in the *right* town, in the *right* state, residential real estate is a gold mine. Again, it's location, location, location that matters. A home in Des Moines, or Peoria, or Baltimore may go down over the long term, but that's because these areas are losing population. Therefore, demand does not exceed supply. But over the next decade, homes in fast-growing red states are going up—*way up.*

Now go a step further. Pick the best street in the best part of town (preferably inside a gated community), within the best school district, in red states where you are guaranteed a steady stream of Millionaire Republican buyers and high demand (outpacing supply) for the next decade or longer. The result is that in most decades you will make a bloody fortune. And the bonus is that up to $500,000 of that fortune is *tax free.* No other investment can do that for you. Uncle Sam is literally giving away money. And when that happens, grab with both hands! The principal residence mortgage deduction and the $500,000 tax exemption is available to every American. I guarantee you that every Millionaire Republican (in a red state) is taking advantage. Are you?

Secret # 2A:
Own More *Republican Red Real Estate*

One of the things author Kiyosaki of *Rich Dad, Poor Dad* was dead *right* about is the idea of owning real estate that pays you an income stream: rental property. Where I take exception with him is that you and your family should *not* live in a small, old, creaky, leaky dump so you can save enough money to buy that investment property. Not only is it a miserable, depressing way to live, but as I've just explained above, it is financially foolish! Your main investment, even before your rental property, should be your home—the bigger and more expensive, the better. Now, with that said, I totally agree with Kiyosaki that you must strive to own even more real estate (but only in red states). Even if you have to get a second job, third job, second mortgage, or a home equity line of credit (which you can do more often in red states because of the fast appreciation), you should be buying rental property as often as humanly possible. Just buying a small rental unit (perhaps a condo or ski cabin) every other year means that at the end of twenty years, you'll own ten investment properties—*plus* your principal residence. And that's a worst-case scenario. If you took my advice and bought the biggest house possible in a hot market in a red state, you'll probably earn that $500,000 tax-free profit several times over the next twenty years—thereby enabling you to buy many additional investment properties! And once you've gained some experience doing it, you'll probably have sold a few of your investment properties at a hefty profit, too (paying only 15 percent capital gains tax, or zero tax if you make a tax-free exchange), enabling you to buy even more real estate or invest in your own business. With the tax money you'll be saving and the higher appreciation in the red states where you're living and investing, you should be able to own fifteen to twenty or more income-producing properties over the next twenty years. Do you know what that means? You're rich! *Filthy rich.* Your retirement is set and worry-free. You don't even need to sell these properties. You can live off the rental income for the rest of your life (paying low or no state income tax because you chose to live in a red state). And when you die in your red state, your kids will owe lower or no state inheritance taxes. Isn't red a fabulous color? God bless the Republican Party!

Again, any smart financial guru can advise you to acquire rental properties. My more important advice is to buy rental properties only in hot markets in red states. The difference in appreciation will be startling—perhaps enough to pay for an extra rental property every second or third year for the next twenty years. Trust me, your kids and grandkids will thank Uncle Wayne—your favorite Millionaire Republican!

Secret # 3: Own Real Estate in International Tax Havens

In today's world, Millionaire Republicans must think globally. The fact is, America has become a high-tax country. Even those Republican red states I've spoken glowingly about throughout this book still tax their residents (through sales tax, property tax, and other stealth taxes) at much higher rates than foreign tax havens. And the residents of those red states still pay ridiculously high federal income tax, FICA tax, Medicare tax, and more. That's why investing in foreign tax havens is such a brilliant strategy—the low-tax or no-tax structures in these places are attracting record numbers of wealthy retirees. Europeans have been moving to low-tax havens for years to escape high taxes. More recently, American retirees have been joining the exodus. I predict that what has been a "trickle" will soon become a "flood" as the Baby Boom generation chooses to retire *outside* the United States. Liberal Democrats will be mystified that Americans will be willing (actually anxious) to flee America for virtually unknown "backwards" foreign countries. To paraphrase James Carville, "It's the taxes, stupid!" Millions of upper-income Boomers will retire to places like Belize, Panama, Costa Rica, Nicaragua, Ecuador, the Cayman Islands, Bahamas, Anguilla, Nevis, Andorra, Malta, Cyprus, Eastern Europe, and the Balkans. These are places where Baby Boomer retirees can live like millionaires on a limited income. The dollar goes farther and tax rates are zero (or close to it). They can sell their homes here in America, replace them with homes on beaches or mountaintops, at half the price (or less), and hire a household staff for pennies on the dollar. And I'm not talking about the truly wealthy retirees with $10 million or more—they're going to retire and live wherever they want and however they want. I'm talking about the tens of millions of Baby Boomers who are going to retire with their life savings of $1 to $2 million (primarily due to the appreciation of their homes, which they are going to sell to fund their retirement). They'll use 10 to 20 percent to buy a nicer home offshore and live like royalty—*tax free*—on the balance. The bad news for America, and an issue I've not heard anyone else address, is that trillions of dollars will disappear from the American economy, along with billions from the tax system. It's bad news because the younger generation left behind is going to be facing a smaller domestic economy and an even larger tax burden. The good news for all you reading this book is that you now know how to capitalize! Just like my advice above, to invest only in red states, here you have an opportunity to invest in low-tax countries—where demand once again outstrips supply (because of the low taxes). Real estate values will go up far more dramatically in Panama, Cyprus, Belize, or Cayman than anywhere in Canada, England, France, or Italy. Liberals just don't get it—taxes destroy our quality of life and ruin our standard of living, especially for retirees. As Europeans have been doing for years, Americans will vote with their feet and move in ever greater numbers to tax havens in exotic places across the globe. That will turn investing in real estate in these offshore tax and retirement havens into one of the most profitable investments of this century—whether you choose to stay in America or become an expat yourself.

I want to make it very clear that *nothing* in this book is meant in any way to be tax advice, and I would certainly never advocate anyone not paying every cent of tax due. As an American citizen you are required to report and pay income taxes (subject to certain exemptions) to the U.S. government no matter where you live and no matter where your money is invested or earned. I won't even begin to argue how ridiculous that is—other than pointing out that it is exactly the equivalent of the State of New York demanding that I pay income taxes to New York State for the rest of my life, simply because I was born there! But I will point out that as a practical matter, with their homes, money, and lives all in another country (other than pension and Social Security funds received from the U.S. government), income reported and taxes paid will be at the discretion of the taxpayer, with *no* practical way of enforcement.

Secret # 4: Own *Your Own Business or Career*

Remember when I said in Chapter Two, "The Divided States of America," that America is now divided between owners and renters? Well, the idea of owning versus renting applies to more than just your home and real estate—it applies most importantly to your *career!* Republicans, especially Millionaire Republicans, choose to *own* instead of rent their careers, too. They understand that only from risk comes reward. What the liberal media often calls the division between the "haves" and the "have nots" is actually a division between the risk-takers and the play-it-safers. Robert Kiyosaki called people like this "Rich Dad" versus "Poor Dad." He described "Rich Dad" as an independent-minded, risk-taking business owner. Meanwhile, "Poor Dad" was a government employee and union member who relied on a "safe weekly paycheck." Of course, "safe" is a relative word. That supposedly safe paycheck left "Poor Dad" broke, bitter, fearful about his future, and reliant on government to survive his retirement. The risks taken by "Rich Dad" left him wealthy and independent. "Rich Dad's" future wasn't reliant on a measly Social Security check. Most Americans fall into that same great financial divide between those who think of themselves as owners (entrepreneurs, small-business owners, business executives, independent contractors, performance-based sales executives, and professionals), versus those with an employee mentality (people who rely on "big brother"—a boss, a big company, a sugar daddy, a union, or a government program to pay their bills). Again, it's the difference between owning and renting.

There is no more important secret for me to teach you in this book than the idea of owning your own business. I call this age in which we are living "The Century of Individuality and Independence." You know individuality is a hot trend when the

United States Army uses "An Army of One" as its advertising slogan! Personally, I don't see anything about joining the army that reminds me of individuality or independence. To me, the Army is all about becoming part of a team and *losing* your individuality. Everyone dresses exactly the same, has the same bad haircut, receives the same basic training, receives the same pay, and takes orders from superiors. Does that sound like individuality to you? Yet even the U.S. Army had no choice but to stress the idea of individuality. Nothing could be a better example of the importance individuality plays in the American psyche of the twenty-first century than the U.S. military recognizing its need to change their image or perish! Independence, free thinking, and personal responsibility are hot trends that will dominate American society (and business) for many years to come. "If it is to be, it is up to me!" is the new mantra. It should be your mantra, too.

How do you take advantage of this crucial trend? Simple: Become a risk-taker! Start your own business. Don't depend on government. Don't depend on a boss. Depend only on yourself (and trusted business partners). The only way to gain financial independence in America today is to take chances. You must be willing to risk your assets to start a business and therefore *own* your career. "Starting a business" means creating any source of income where you are in control, and as your business or performance improves, you gain the lion's share of the compensation and appreciation (i.e., ownership). Professionals and salespeople provide good examples of "starting your own business" and controlling your own destiny: lawyers, doctors, accountants, architects, contractors, stockbrokers, real estate brokers, real estate appraisers, mortgage brokers, investment bankers, financial planners, business consultants, self-employed independent contractors, and other kinds of commission-based sales jobs (where you are *paid for performance*). Of course, it also can mean starting a business like a retail store, restaurant, or franchise. More Americans than ever before depend on themselves—not a boss, not a big company, not a union, not a government. And these business owners and performance-based earners are the highest earners in our society—by far! They are the backbone of the Republican Party and the backbone of the American economy (small business has created over 70 percent of all new jobs in the last decade).

As an example, the reason Las Vegas has been number one in America for so many consecutive years in population growth, job growth, building permits, and just about every other category of business success is that it is number one in America in entrepreneurship. Las Vegas was America's fastest-growing market for small-business growth between 1998 and 2003, adding almost 30,000 small businesses during that period. That adds up to a 58.5 percent increase (nineteen percentage points higher than the number-two city). That might be why a panel of economic experts in *USA Today* recently called Las Vegas "the economic engine of America and Wall Street." Business growth, economic success, entrepreneurship, and low taxes are what create Millionaire Republicans. They go together like apple pie, motherhood, and the good old USA! The America of the future is truly an army of one!

Owning your own business is not just about being the boss, or building financial freedom, or controlling your future. Those are all big benefits, but owning your own business is also very much about controlling and limiting taxes. Let me be blunt—as an employee, you are *screwed!* By the time you get your "safe paycheck," the government has already grabbed their share. (You have no say in this little matter—even though it's your money.) But as a "business owner" you control what comes through your door and have the right to decide how to spend it. If you choose, you can "reinvest" it in your business—buy more supplies, hire more employees, increase advertising and marketing, or expand your operations. At the end of the year, if you reinvested all of it for legitimate business expenses, you may find you owe little or no income tax! By reinvesting your profits, you have a unique ability to both legally shelter your income and grow your assets, *tax free* (because as your business increases in value, you owe no taxes until the day you sell). And once you do sell your business, you pay federal capital gains taxes of only 15 percent (and zero state taxes in many red states), instead of the 40 percent and higher rates (including FICA) imposed on "earned" income. Once again, you can thank the GOP for that crucial tax break for investors and business owners—it has always been Republican politicians who have fought for lower capital gains taxes to reward business owners for the risks they take and the jobs they create. These are the critical tax advantages of owning a business versus collecting a "safe" weekly paycheck as an employee. Millionaire Republicans understand the advantage of using a business structure to shield assets and reduce taxes.

Of course, the biggest advantage of all is simple and has nothing to do with taxes. By definition, the only way a business can succeed and stay in business is if it earns more from the labor of its employees than it pays them. Therefore, as an employee, no one can ever pay you what you are worth but *you*. Your employer may pay you enough to survive, buy a Saturn, and pay the rent. But only by working for yourself will you be compensated enough to buy a Mercedes and a mansion on a golf course. That's the advantage of owning versus renting your career—you are in control. That's why so many smart Millionaire Republicans choose to own their own businesses.

I hate to sound like a broken record . . . but the same advice for owning your home or investment property also holds for owning your business. *Do it in a red state!* Why? For the exact same reasons: The opportunity is greater simply because that's where the people and dollars are going. Yes, you can make a bloody fortune by owning the right business in New York or California. But your start-up and operating costs are far higher (because of taxes, burdensome rules and regulations, and far more expensive employee requirements like health insurance and workers' comp). Your audience is shrinking in blue states—meaning you are always competing for a piece of a smaller and smaller customer base. And upon selling your business, you'll be taxed at a far higher rate in a blue state (thereby threatening your retirement plans). The bottom line is that your margin for error is much slimmer in California, New York, or any other high-tax blue state, versus fast-growing, low-tax, lower-cost red states.

One last aside: Being older is no longer an excuse for "playing it safe." More and more older Americans are thinking like Millionaire Republicans. New research shows that because of corporate layoffs, entrepreneurship is actually growing *faster* among older workers than any other age group! Almost six million Americans age fifty and older now own their own businesses—a twenty-three percent jump from 1990. Bet on this trend to grow even hotter as more workers realize that corporations want to slash payrolls, cut jobs, and relocate jobs overseas—all as the ranks of Americans age fifty and older rise dramatically to 118 million by 2020. Older Americans are the perfect entrepreneurs: They already possess business experience; they are disciplined and reliable; they aren't afraid of hard work; they have time to dedicate to building a business because their children are already grown; and they have saved the kind of money necessary to bankroll a business. Because of the maverick personality of this Baby Boom generation and the unique situation currently developing, I believe America (and the world) is about to experience historic levels of entrepreneurship. And that, of course, will lead to more Republican voters and contributors. The "Century of Individuality and Independence" goes hand in hand with the Red Storm!

Secret # 5: *Whatever You Own, You Must* Sell

This secret is simple and straightforward. To own your own business or career (and to earn big dollars), *you must learn the art of salesmanship.* You've heard it said of most successful people that "He's a natural born salesman." Donald Trump certainly has that skill. So does Richard Branson, Warren Buffett (or didn't you notice that that "aw shucks" style is part of the sale?), Ross Perot (he almost sold America on a third-party presidency), and Steve Wynn (who sold Wall Street investors on supplying $2.7 billion to build the most expensive hotel in the world). Bobby Flay and Emeril, the stars of The Food Channel, can sell even better than they cook! There are thousands of great chefs in America—yet only a handful become TV stars with restaurants across the country. What is the difference between a short-order cook and Bobby Flay? About $20 million! But what's important is how Bobby managed to turn his talent into a million-dollar empire—the guy can *sell.* That's how you build a business empire—with top-notch sales and promotional skills! Look at hairstylists. On every block, in every town, there is a small barbershop or a Super Cuts franchise. The barbers in these salons get paid $8 or $10 per hour (plus tips). But turn your TV dial to QVC or the Home Shopping Network. There you'll find "hairstylists" earning millions of dollars selling their own products. Or go to a high-class hair salon—Christophe,

Jose Eber, Vidal Sassoon, Frederic Fekkai, and Sally Hershberger charge $500 or more for a cut and style, while the barbers down the block charge $20. What's the difference? Salesmanship! The stylists-turned-TV-celebrities *sell*, market, and promote themselves better.

Sales and promotion are the determining factors for virtually every successful businessperson, politician, entrepreneur, Hollywood mogul, and even religious leader! You don't think ministers sell? The most successful religious leaders of our time were Reverends Billy Graham, Robert Schuller, and Norman Vincent Peale. They all preached the same God, the same Bible, and the same biblical principles. What separated these TV evangelists from all the other anonymous ministers of the world? How did they become celebrities, while others just like them toiled in poverty and obscurity? The answer is obvious: Graham, Schuller, and Peale were all consummate *salesmen*. And, it worked—they converted millions of Americans to Christianity while building multimillion-dollar TV and publishing empires. Salesmanship is the way you convert clients—or Christians!

How about authors like yours truly? Well, there's good reason why authors call our measurement of success "the best-*seller* list." There is no designation as "best" without *selling*. Sales is the key to being the best in the publishing business—just like in every other business. Do you know what you call a talented writer with a great story but no sales ability? An *unpublished* author.

Do football coaches need to sell? I'm proud to say Coach Ron Meyer is a good friend of mine. He is a former College Coach of the Year and a two-time American Football Conference Coach of the Year (for the Colts and the Patriots). Does he know his X's and O's? Sure, all football coaches know "the playbook." But what truly separates the winners from the losers is salesmanship! The best coaches are master motivators (through sales, they convince their players that they really can win) and master recruiters (they hit the road to sell recruits and their parents on their football program). Ron Meyer is one of the best salesmen I've ever met. Football coaching isn't just about X's and O's. It also takes a big smile, a firm handshake, and a great pep talk before the game and at halftime. Vince Lombardi was a salesman just as much as a coach. That could be why his football quotes are still used by virtually every business speaker and sales motivator today—forty years later!

You show me someone who doesn't sell for a living (and faces no risk) and I'll show you someone who doesn't make big money. Librarians don't sell; neither do teachers or college professors, butchers or bakers, plumbers or electricians, construction workers or truck drivers, firemen, policemen, or paramedics, government bureaucrats or union members, secretaries or middle managers at big corporations, maids or front-desk clerks or just about anybody in this world who collects a "safe paycheck" once a week. It is interesting to note that the few people in these occupations who are talented at the art of salesmanship quickly move up to be the bosses, or go off and start their own businesses.

So what do most of the people I listed above have in common? They are almost all loyal lifelong Democratic voters. They are nice, salt-of-the-earth people. But they were never taught the importance of sales as the key to success and wealth, and unfortunately, since so many of them are teachers and professors, they teach the wrong message to our children, too. The result is that they are forever broke and dissatisfied (remember "Poor Dad") and don't know why. They are angry and jealous of those who earn the big bucks. If only they understood that the only difference between a life of boredom, misery, mediocrity, and financial inferiority, versus a life of excitement, wealth, ownership, and financial freedom is that dirty little word: *salesmanship.* The salaried employees and union members of the world never learned how to sell; they never learned the importance of sales to achieving wealth; they think selling is hard work and "bothers" people; and they want a "safe" guaranteed check. Well, for all those reasons they are *screwed.* They have no control over their lives, no upside, no bonuses or commissions, because by taking a salary, they are "capped" or limited in what they can make, with no ownership, so there is nothing to sell when they decide to retire. Why is all this not taught in school? If it were, perhaps our children would have an educated decision to make upon graduation—to sell or not.

Sales is a dirty word to liberals. Whether it be liberals in the media, liberal politicians, or the liberal educators who run our

THE 18 REPUBLICAN SECRETS

schools, they all teach the same message: Selling is bad, low-class, tacky, and offensive. Because of this bias, salesmanship has never been taught in school, and the liberals who determine the education agenda will always keep it that way. Selling may not be an important skill if you're a tenured teacher with no chance of losing your job—if all you have to do is show up at work, go through the motions, and head home at 2 p.m. Sales may be unnecessary to union members, minimum-wage employees, or anyone who simply collects a check and works 9 to 5. But if you want more out of life than a "safe" job and a mediocre paycheck, if you want to *own* your job or career, you'd better learn to sell! The best-paying jobs in America involve sales and come with no guarantees! They are all performance-based. *You perform, or you don't eat.* There is an important lesson to be learned here: If you're uncomfortable selling or unwilling to take risks, the odds are you'll never become a Millionaire Republican.

Liberal Democrats also hate sales because they are afraid of risk and competition. They value safety, even if it means everyone shares in *mediocrity.* It's why they want to tax the wealthy so heavily—to redistribute the wealth and create "fairness" and equality. That way, there are no winners or losers (no competition)—everyone lives a mediocre but "fair" life. It's why liberals support a nationalized health care system and fear the privatization of Social Security. They'd rather accept the security of mediocrity than take any risk on a much more abundant future. The sales world is competitive, risky, tough, "dog eat dog." If you don't perform, you don't get paid. Liberals are scared to death of the idea of anyone losing their job due to mediocre performance. That's why the liberal politicians and union leaders fight so hard to make sure teacher pay is based on length of service but never on performance. But they have it all wrong. It's Liberal Democrats who have created the Divided States of America with this flawed thinking. They are the ones to blame for the poverty and hopelessness of their own voters. The people who think like Liberal Democrats are unprepared for competition. They have the wrong set of skills and wrong mind-set. So the "play it safers" fail in the competitive private sector, or choose not to compete at all by taking a "safe" job in the public sector. Then they retire into poverty and dependence on a measly Social Security check.

I've repeatedly stressed the Millionaire Republican mantra: "Safety" is bad for you! It limits you. It strangles the life out of you. It destroys ambition and drive. It stifles competition. It leads to the survivor mentality, instead of the *thriver* mentality. Millionaire Republicans are thrivers. We are competitive and aggressive. We want to be rewarded (and are not afraid to be punished) based on our performance. We understand that there are winners and losers. We expect to be the winners and are willing to put our money where are mouths are (by taking risks, starting our own businesses, or being paid by performance). We are ambitious, driven, and hungry. We understand that selling (and selling *well*) is the path to attaining wealth and success. Millionaire Republicans sell every day of our lives. Salesmanship has always been the crucial trait necessary for achieving wealth. But it is more important today than ever before, simply because we are living in a more entrepreneurial age (as well as one dominated by marketing, public relations, and instant gratification).

So now you know the three crucial secrets to becoming a Millionaire Republican: owning, risking, and selling! Virtually everything I'll teach you in this book has one or all of these three concepts at its root (excuse the pun).

One last postscript: How crucial is salesmanship to politics? It is the determining factor in why Republicans have dominated presidential politics for almost forty years! Richard Nixon was certainly a better salesman than either Hubert Humphrey or George McGovern. Ronald Reagan outsold Jimmy Carter and Walter Mondale by a mile. The elder George Bush badly outsold Michael Dukakis (actually embarrassed him). And George W. Bush outsold two boring, stiff Democratic candidates: Al Gore and John Kerry. What did all those Democratic presidential losers have in common? They were all nice men, decent human beings, and salt-of-the-earth Americans. But they all had very bland personalities and absolutely *no* salesmanship skills. None of them could sell their vision or political platform to the people. But can you name the one Democrat who broke through? Bill Clinton—perhaps the best salesman out of all the modern American presidents. Bill had the crucial trait that most Liberal Democrats lack—the ability to smile, shake hands, remember names, speak with confidence and charisma, and *sell* himself to the public. Perhaps more Liberal Democrats need to learn this crucial trait instead of looking down their noses at it.

Salesmanship is the very reason Republicans will continue to dominate American politics for many years to come.

Secret # 6: Own *Your Future* by Owning *Your Time*

Millionaire Republicans are not sitting around waiting for Social Security. We have no interest in surviving on a measly one thousand to two thousand dollars a month. We are thrivers, even in retirement. The way to own, not rent, your future is to own your time. And what should you do with that time? *Sell some more!* Millionaire Republicans are human dynamos. (I call them living, breathing Energizer Bunnies!) They are not satisfied working only 9 to 5. They take action to find a second or even third income stream to build their nest egg for retirement. They also understand the power of *owning* versus renting. Most people who work for a "safe" paycheck at their primary job unfortunately choose a "safe" paycheck for their second job too (driving a cab, working at a deli, working as a part-time bookkeeper, substitute teacher, etc.). That adds a minimum wage or slightly higher to their income. At that rate, they'll break their backs just to add a few thousand dollars to their savings. One accident or illness and all that extra money is wiped out in an instant. When it comes to your first job, the choice of playing it safe is downright foolish. But when it comes to a second career, choosing safety again is just plain deadly. Millionaire Republicans understand that you get rich only through sales. So even if you choose to collect a "safe" paycheck in your main career (in order to pay the bills), listen to this advice carefully: *You must choose a performance-based job for your second career.* Sell real estate on weekends. Become a financial planner in your spare time. Open a small business (and hire a manager to run it 9 to 5). Build a multi-level marketing (MLM) sales business such as Amway, Mary Kay Cosmetics, or Herbalife. Even if you're a teacher or professor full-time at your day job, you can build an MLM career (in MLM each person owns his or her own home-based business) on the side, all the while paying the bills with your "safe" job.

I've heard Liberal Democrats laughing and criticizing MLM sales businesses my whole life. Remember, liberals think selling is low class—it's *beneath* them. "Poor Dad" certainly would have scoffed at "lowering himself" to selling MLM products such as Amway out of his home. Well, I personally know countless Americans who earn six-figure incomes off MLM sales. I have several friends who have earned seven-figure incomes off MLM careers! My own father-in-law worked twelve- to fourteen-hour days as a hospital CEO (responsible for more than 600 employees) for thirty years, all the while using his "spare time" to build an Amway business. The thousands of extra dollars a month he earned from that part-time MLM business helped pay for my wife's college education and his retirement. Interestingly, as a success and motivational speaker, I've addressed several large MLM conventions and had the honor of meeting thousands of

MLM business owners. In all these years of meeting thousands of MLMers, I don't believe I've ever met a Democrat—*not one*. Because people who are so driven, ambitious, and success-oriented that they choose to build a second or third business from their home are virtually always Republicans. Rather than complain about how "unfair" life is, they simply choose to work their butts off to get ahead. They choose to *own* their own time. They use every spare second in their lives to own and control their financial futures and build a legacy for their children and grandchildren. Interestingly, that's the kind of mind-set required to become a Millionaire Republican, no matter where you started, no matter how "unfair" life is.

But building a second sales- and performance-based career is only the start. Then you must put that extra income to work—by using every dime from that second or third income stream to buy real estate or stocks (but always buy *red* stocks, or real estate in *red* states). Keep your extra money working for you—even while you sleep. This is how Millionaire Republicans choose to own our spare time and thereby control and own our futures! This is precisely why Democrats live their golden years dependent on Social Security and unable even to afford the rent on their small apartments, while Republicans retire to a life of sailing, golfing, traveling, Mediterranean cruises, owning everything from a home to a vacation home to a motor coach that's the size of a home, and spoiling our grandchildren. We've *earned* it by choosing to own every spare minute of our time (and using that time to sell and own)!

Secret # 7: Own Republican Red Stocks

The two most prevalent ways to build wealth in America have always been investing in real estate and stocks. Investing in public companies on Wall Street has historically (despite slumps, crashes, recessions, and even depressions) been a huge winner for Americans—rich, poor, or in-between. The coming decades will be no different. Every aspiring Millionaire Republican should make stocks a significant part of his investment and retirement portfolio. So what stocks do I recommend? You guessed it—*Republican red stocks!* Successful stock picking is about predicting tomorrow's winners today. If the coming years (and decades) will be dominated by a Republican Red Storm, then it makes sense to buy stocks that will benefit from this historic realignment. Picking Wall Street winners is as simple as understanding Republican red trends.

MORE AMERICANS THAN EVER
WILL BE BUYING STOCKS.

The tax cuts on dividends and capital gains instituted by President George W. Bush make owning stocks more profitable and therefore bode well for stocks as a profitable investment choice for years to come. The biggest bonus of all time would be the privatization of Social Security in some form (even if it's only private add-ons). It may take a few years, but some form of privatization is inevitable (it just makes too much economic sense). With this change will come even more opportunity to profit on Wall Street. But with or without privatization, red stocks are a big winner for the foreseeable future. The immediate beneficiaries of this surge in stock-buying will be Wall Street and the publicly traded financial services companies: Merrill Lynch, Charles Schwab, Bear Stearns, Morgan Stanley, Goldman Sachs, Lehman Brothers, UBS, Raymond James, AG Edwards, etc. And as the Internet continues to become a part of our everyday lives, so will buying stocks online. Therefore, I recommend making a bet on online brokerage leaders like E*TRADE and TDAmeritrade. The other reason to invest in stockbrokerage companies is that Republican dominance goes hand in hand with sales success (remember, Republicans like to sell). If sales are king in this century, then the "king of sales" is the stockbrokerage business. So owning stock in brokerage firms is a solid bet on two hot long-term trends—stocks and sales.

MORE AMERICANS THAN EVER WILL BE BUYING HOMES.

Therefore, I'd make an investment in the biggest publicly traded developers/home builders, contractors, building materials suppliers, mortgage companies, title companies, real estate brokerages, and home security firms. Could there be a real estate downturn short-term? Absolutely. I'd actually say a real estate bust is likely. But all of my advice is long-term. Long-term, real estate in red states will continue appreciating dramatically. As a result, I wouldn't bet on just any builder or realtor. I'd make my bet on companies that do most of their business in red states. A home builder in Las Vegas, Reno, Austin, Dallas, Scottsdale, Palm Beach, or Boise is a much better investment than a home builder counting on continued growth in New York, Baltimore, Boston, or Philadelphia. Remember, Millionaire Republicans and aspiring Millionaire Republicans are moving in droves to the South and the West. That's where the money is and therefore where the most successful companies in the housing and real estate development business will be found for many years to come.

THIS PERFECT RED STORM
AFFECTS MEDIA STOCKS TOO.

All these Republican-leaning home owners, stock owners, and business owners do more than vote Republican—they also *watch* and listen Republican! This new "ownership society" craves more conservative news and talk. That's precisely why the FOX News Channel now dominates over all other cable news channels. The big news stars are Republican TV talkers like Bill O'Reilly and Sean Hannity. The renters of the world watch CNN, PBS, MSNBC, and other liberal media outlets. But those who *own and invest* watch FOX News Channel (and go to FOXNews.com) and CNBC. Soon they'll be watching FOX Business (a new cable channel expected to start in early 2006). Therefore, I believe the best "red stock play" in the media sector is to bet on the continued growth of conservative news and entertainment with News Corporation, FOX Entertainment Group, and Clear Channel Radio (owners of most of the conservative talk radio stations).

GAMING STOCKS ARE A "BEST BET"!

Many on the Christian right, who so often vote Republican, think of gambling as a sin. *I do not.* Gambling is as natural to Americans as eating and sleeping. Betting on a stock on Wall Street is just as much about gambling as betting on red or black, poker, or blackjack. Betting on IBM or Microsoft online at Charles Schwab or E*TRADE is not much different from betting on the Yankees, the Los Angeles Lakers, or the Dallas Cowboys at an online sportsbook (neither of which should be done, at a serious level, without professional advice). Americans love to gamble. And a certain group of Americans loves to gamble more than any other—"rainmakers" (entrepreneurs, business owners, and sales leaders). I've talked again and again about the dramatic growth of sales and entrepreneurship in this century. Entrepreneurs and salespeople are born risk-takers. They enjoy the thrill ride that comes from risking assets, starting a business, or making sales calls to total strangers. That thrill doesn't end at the office. Business risk-takers are also big gamblers. They love Las Vegas. They'll bet on anything that moves. This American gambling frenzy has made possible the overnight success of two relatively new forms of gambling: tribal casinos and online gambling. As the ranks of business owners and salespeople grow and prosper in this Red Storm, you can bet they will be gambling with both fists at casinos, sportsbooks, racetracks, tribal casinos, poker rooms, online casinos—in short, *if it moves, they'll bet on it.* Therefore, my "best bets" are Las Vegas and publicly traded gaming companies. I predict gaming giants like Harrah's, MGM Mirage, Sands Las Vegas, Wynn Resorts, Boyd Gaming, Stations Casinos, and IGT will be long-term Wall Street darlings. Smart Millionaire Republicans will be betting with both fists on Vegas and the gaming industry to thrive!

I also am a big believer (and bettor) in the global growth of online gaming. Remarkably, 39 percent of all money spent online by Europeans is spent on gambling. But that's *small* compared to the dollars being bet online by Americans. Despite the fact that online gaming is considered illegal in this country, as much as half of all the money wagered online is being bet by American citizens. It's the new Prohibition! Politicians, wake up—the genie is out of the bottle. Prohibition was a miserable failure the first time—this time will be no different. Online gambling cannot be stopped or even slowed. Tens of billions of dollars bet online will soon become hundreds of billions, and eventually *trillions.* Internet gambling is the perfect bet on tech-nology in the twenty-first century.

My prediction is that some form of online gaming, probably poker, will be legalized, regulated, and taxed here in America in the near future. And the success of that limited form of online gaming will lead to full legalization (and taxation) of online gaming within the next decade. Whatever your moral views of gambling, there is no doubt that online gaming is a gold mine and that the need for ever higher tax revenues by American politicians will overcome the moral arguments against it in a few short years. So bet on the legalization of online gaming in America. Who will be the biggest beneficiaries? The odds are the leaders in this new field will be the current Vegas-based leaders of land-based gaming named above. But just in case I'm wrong and the head start handed out to global gaming companies proves too powerful to overcome, I'd make a hedge bet on the current industry leaders traded publicly on the British stock exchanges: Hilton Group (owners of Ladbrokes), SportingBet, Aristocrat at Gaming (Australian-based) William Hill, BetonSports, Gaming Corp., NetTeller (a money-transfer service for online gaming transactions), and British Sky Broadcasting (owners of BSkyB, where viewers can place bets on their TV screens), among others. WPT Enterprises (owners of the World Poker Tour) and Party Gaming (owner of Party Poker) may also be good bets due to the amazing popularity of poker sweeping the globe.

I also predict that a Republican-dominated future will be

profitable for defense, health care, pharmaceutical, and energy stocks.

You get the picture—*bet on red!* Liberal Democrats claim that Wall Street is only for the "rich." They also claim that any privatization of Social Security will only help Wall Street fat cats and big business, at the expense of ordinary Americans. Nonsense! Who do you think owns all these stocks on Wall Street? I'll tell you who—America! Due to the popularity of mutual funds, IRAs, SEP IRAs, college funds, and other forms of retirement accounts, stock ownership is no longer just for the rich. The average middle-class American who owns mutual funds and retirement accounts now has a huge stake in Wall Street. Therefore, the success of public companies (which liberals derogatorily call "big business") helps *all* Americans. Middle-class Americans no longer see Wall Street as "big business" or "the enemy." They now root for Wall Street simply because they want their stocks to go up! Democrats just don't get it; as Calvin Coolidge first reported a hundred years ago, "The business of America is business!"

Secret # 7a: Own *More Red Stocks* (as in China)

I've recommended that Americans move west and south to capitalize on the Red Storm. But when it comes to stocks, you'll also need to head east—to China. There is no question that China is well on its way to becoming the dominant producer, consumer, and economic power in the world. As much as I believe in the greatness of America and Americans, I must admit that the future of the world's economy in this century belongs to China. This insight provides a great opportunity for you to profit. But most Americans (as usual) will sit back and watch it happen—without ever making a dime. Here is another thing that separates the American masses from Millionaire Republicans. The masses are either unwilling to accept the fact that it's a big world out there and America is not the only country thriving (willingness to accept change is an important Republican rule), or they are afraid to make investments outside their own country (willingness to risk is also an important Republican rule). No Millionaire Republican will let ignorance or fear stop him from profiting on this explosive trend.

Steve Wynn, one of the most brilliant businessmen of our generation and one of my personal heroes, recently reported to the *Las Vegas Review Journal* on what he sees when he gets off the plane in China. Wynn said, "You travel halfway around the world, you get off the plane and you're in San Diego. *They are us.* The only difference when you walk down the street, [is that] the cities are the size of Chicago. There are fifty cities in China the size of Chicago and New York." Enough said! The two most successful and brilliant visionaries in Las Vegas are Steve Wynn and Sheldon Adelson, and both are betting big on China by building billion-dollar casino/resorts in Macao. If China is good enough for Wynn and Adelson, it's good enough for me. Recently I've met a number of Chinese businesspeople. They are not just educated, bright, and ambitious. They are hungry—actually *starving*—for success. I love to bet on people who are starving for success and wealth. That's the way America was a hundred years ago before the liberal media and liberal educators created a generation of underachievers, blamers, and complainers, dependent on Big Brother. China, on the other hand, is filled with tens of millions of hungry, hardworking, ambitious entrepreneurs and future millionaires!

My second global investment choice, right behind China, is India. I know, you think of India as a country full of hundreds of millions of poor people—and it is! But India already has a middle class that outnumbers America's entire population! And like China, India is full of educated, hungry, ambitious, industrious, risk-taking dreamers. I always bet my money on people like that. India and China (together with America) are the economic engines of the future. The bonus is that the attitudes of people in China and India are similar to the mind-set of Millionaire Republicans. I wouldn't bet my money on Europeans. (Or at least not Western Europeans. The youth of Eastern Europe—Hungary, Romania, the Czech Republic, Russia, Ukraine, and the Balkans are as hungry as their Chinese and Indian counterparts—there just aren't nearly as many of them.) Western Europeans are negative and suspicious toward wealth, and hung up on petty jealousy, bitterness, and anger toward America. They have become the mirror image of Liberal Democrats. They are the new "global liberals." While Chinese and Indians crave wealth and material possessions (just like Millionaire Republicans), Western Europeans spend their time complaining, protesting, and demanding more government entitlements and longer guaranteed vacations. Meanwhile, the Chinese and Indians want to either emulate America, immigrate to America, or beat our pants off. I respect that attitude! China and India have the mind-set and hunger to join America as global economic leaders. My advice to aspiring Millionaire Republicans is to head east—by buying stock in the success of China and India.

Secret # 8: Own *Your Children's Education* *(and Their Future)*

I constantly hear liberals say that most parents cannot afford private school. First, that statement is erroneous—it just depends upon your *priorities.* My father was a butcher, my mom a homemaker. Yet they scraped together enough money to send me to private high school back in 1977. That sacrifice changed my life. I graduated as valedictorian from that private school (Thornton Donovan School, in New Rochelle, New York), was accepted into prestigious Columbia University, and the rest (as they say) is history. I never looked back. I owe all of my success to my parents, my private school education, and the principal of that private school, Doug Fleming. (Today, twenty-five years later, I count Doug as one of my best friends.) My parents' decision to sacrifice to send me to an exclusive private school is called "setting priorities." If parents believe that their children's future is the most important priority in their lives, they will find a way to get their children out of the miserable failure that liberals and greedy teachers' unions (the so-called "education lobbies") have made of the public school system. Please note that I vehemently separate "teachers' unions" from "teachers." Most teachers I have met are bright, dedicated, concerned, and hardworking. Unfortunately, bureaucrats and union opera- tives have taken control of the education system and are milk- ing it for their own power and profit. Their mantra is "Education needs more money!" And what is their argument as to why they need more money? It's because they are *failing!* So they demand to be paid more money for *failing* performance? No wonder they fail: The more they fail, the more money they get paid by taxpayers! The worse the performance gets, the more they demand to be paid! This is undoubtedly the most blatant rip-off of taxpayers in America's history—and it may prove to be the downfall of this great country. It's certainly the downfall of millions of children of poor Democrats. But smart Republicans will not allow their children to fail. They choose either private school, religious school, or homeschooling. That's how you own your children's future. You take the power and control out of the hands of strangers. You choose to take control and ownership yourself.

Given the sorry state of public education, I believe that homeschooling is the educational wave of the future. It costs less than private school, and what could possibly be safer than knowing exactly where your kids are all day long? What could possibly be more effective than intensive one-on-one teaching and training? What could make more sense than relying on teachers who loves their students like their own—because they *are* their own! Would anyone prefer that their kids be taught by strangers, often in dangerous conditions far from home (dilapidated schools, with bullies, gangs, and long bus rides), distracted by classmates with poor habits and low self-esteem, and taught by teachers stretched beyond their limits, aiming for the lowest possible goals as the target?

Too often, kids in public schools are "dumbed down," taught at the lowest level of the worst kids in the classroom. Our public schools are not built or operated for education— they are simply *warehouses* that babysit our children while we are away at work. Schools aren't set up for the good of the students. They are set up to make life as easy as possible for the administrators and the teachers. High school students in Las Vegas start school at 7 a.m. (some have to catch 5:30 a.m. buses)—a ridiculous time for students to try to learn. Perhaps a 7 a.m. start is good for teachers and administrators looking to get the afternoons off, but a 7 a.m. start to the school day makes no sense for children—certainly not if the objective is learning. No wonder our entire public educational system is a miserable failure. News flash: Kids don't learn a thing at 7 a.m. They will learn nothing all day long if you make them get up at 5:30 a.m.

to catch a bus. How utterly ridiculous and *scandalous*. Where are the priorities of the educators?

The proof that homeschooling is a superior alternative is seen in the vicious attacks on it by fearful bureaucrats, teachers' unions, and Liberal Democrat politicians (beholden to teachers' unions) who feel threatened by its success. To give you a personal example, my daughter Dakota just turned thirteen. She has been homeschooled since birth. Since she has been around me 24/7 for the past thirteen years, she already thinks like a Millionaire Republican. She has learned at my side, listened to my business calls, sat in on my business meetings, and debated politics with me since early childhood. Adults who meet Dakota say that she has the maturity and poise of a twentysomething. She can discuss politics, history, and business with any adult. Yet homeschooling doesn't take eight hours a day, five days a week (as public school does). Dakota spends four hours, three times a week with her tutor. She spends the rest of her time reading (as many as a dozen books a week), watching the Learning, History, and Biography Channels, and attending extracurricular activities such as martial arts (Dakota is a year away from her black belt), fencing (she is a competitive fencer who has won numerous tournaments and has set a goal of earning a fencing scholarship to Stanford), tennis, piano, and swimming. Dakota also spends a major portion of her time going on amazing field trips to museums and historical places with her mother and two young brothers (also homeschooled). What a life! She gets to spend her school days around her family, and learn from people who love her dearly and have only her best interests in mind.

Oh, and her grades? Last year Dakota took the Stanford Series 7 exam to test her skills against all sixth-graders across the country. Dakota scored a 99.9 grade in all categories (the highest possible score), along with a designation of PHS, which means she tested at the *post*–high school level in the sixth grade! Let's compare her remarkable success to our failing public schools, where up to 50 percent of minority kids in places like New York City and Los Angeles drop out of high school, and those who do manage to survive until senior year can't even pass a basic skills test (that has been dumbed down so that *anyone* should be able to pass). And then, even the kids who do pass are often forced to take remedial courses in basic English and math during their freshman year at college. Yes, public school students earn high school diplomas and get accepted into college *without* even knowing how to speak, spell, or add at basic levels. Yet my homeschooled daughter in sixth grade had *post*–high school skills!

My advice to all aspiring Millionaire Republicans: Take control and *ownership* of your children's education. Sacrifice time, money, effort—whatever is required to get your kids out of government-run public schools. Your only good choices are private school, religious school, or homeschooling. And if for any reason those choices are not an option for you, then sacrifice time, money, and effort to be involved with your local public schools. Confront them! Do *not* let them tell you they are doing the best they can when they are clearly failing! Get your kids into the magnet, honors, and advanced-placement classes. Don't accept their excuses as to why your child should stay in a failing classroom. And one final note to all you parents (especially of boys): Do *not* allow your son (or daughter) to be classified as ADHD and given drugs! This is one of the most insidious scams perpetrated by school bureaucrats and teachers' unions on our children. They have basically "outlawed" being a boy— you know, squirming, fidgeting, daydreaming, harmless horsing around. Today they call it "ADHD." And do you know why? The schools get more money for every kid they classify that way! Don't let one of them be yours! If you think your child has a true learning disability, get him tested by an independent professional whom you trust. Do not rely on some school psychologist (who is rewarded for labeling and drugging your child) or some twenty-five-year-old teacher who doesn't have any sons of her own and therefore doesn't know what just plain "being a boy" is all about.

If you want your kids to succeed in life, to even have a shot at becoming Millionaire Republicans, those are your only choices. My amazing parents, David and Stella Root, understood that back in 1977. Putting me into Thornton Donovan changed my attitude, mind-set, and life. Public schools are dramatically worse today. And even in "good" schools, do not forget that most teachers think like "Poor Dad." That is not the attitude you want your children to learn. If your future depends on owning versus renting, then the future of your children depends on your owning (and taking personal responsibility for) their education and their future!

Secret # 9: Own *Your Own Education* (*and Personal Growth*)

This Millionaire Republican secret is not about my education at Columbia University, or any other college for that matter. The truth is that Columbia, Harvard, or Stanford all look impressive on your résumé and open lots of doors. That's great, and that's why I'll gladly fork over $250,000 (or more) for a degree from one of those institutions of higher learning for my children. But as far as real world (or business world) knowledge, you're not going to get it at any Ivy League institution (or any other college). The truth is, I learned nothing at Columbia that enabled me to achieve wealth or success in the real world. You heard me—*nothing!* That's why you meet "book smart" people every day who earn mediocre incomes ("Poor Dad"), and "street smart" people who lack formal education and who achieve wealth, fame, and success ("Rich Dad").

We witnessed those same results on NBC's *The Apprentice* when Donald Trump pitted a group of Ivy League whiz kids versus a bunch of high school grads who had achieved high levels of success in the real world. The uneducated "street smart" group more than held their own against the snobby college kids. Of course, the truth is that you'd be better off with *both*. I want my daughter Dakota to attend Stanford and get that impressive degree on her résumé. But, just as important, I'll also make sure that she learns "street smarts." What an unbeatable, lethal combination! But even if you don't have that college sheepskin, you can educate and enlighten yourself every day of the week. Street smarts come from four sources: experience, mentors, role models, and research.

EXPERIENCE

I keep a sign on my wall that says "Everything is easy when you know what to do." Knowing what to do comes only from experience, and unfortunately experience takes time. Here are a few clues to how to maximize that time. Whatever you do, do it to the best of your ability. Whether you start in the boardroom or the mail room, always give 180 percent. *Always have an owner's mentality,* not a renter's mentality. Treat that job (even a menial one) like you own it—as if it is your own business. Listen, observe, and always do *more* than is expected. Work longer hours than are expected. There is a saying, "You have to pay your dues." In this book, I continually stress the need to start your own business. However, that doesn't mean you shouldn't work (and get paid by someone else) while you gain the experience to be ready to go out on your own. But while you're collecting that paycheck working for others, be sure to treat your job

like you own it. Thinking like an owner will lead to your success at anything you do.

MENTORING

Mentoring goes hand in hand with experience. Here's a secret.
Most Millionaire Republicans get a kick out of teaching, training, and mentoring aspiring Millionaire Republicans. It makes
us feel young, smart, and charitable! We especially love to help
people who are willing to help themselves. Doug Miller, my
mentor, always said that he never hesitated to help me for two
reasons: first, because I was smart enough to ask (and ask a lot),
while few others ever did; and second, because I was such an
ambitious and eager student. I'd absorb his advice like a sponge,
apply it, and always say "Thank you," and then I would come
back a day or two later and say, "Okay, I did all that, *now what?*"
Doug says that to this day he never met anyone else as hungry
or ambitious as me. I always chose working, studying, and
learning over partying. Wealth was my goal, and I was willing
to make any sacrifice to achieve it. That's the way all aspiring
Millionaire Republicans must think. That's the kind of *discipline*
necessary to achieve success. If you're not willing to choose
work and learning over partying, don't complain when you
wind up in a dead-end job with mediocre pay.

Doug's mentoring was a key factor in my success. But think
how many others missed out simply because they never both-

ered to ask for Doug's help. My point is, when you meet someone who you think can help you, don't hesitate to *ask.* They will
undoubtedly say yes. Then be sure their advice isn't wasted—
own it! Then come back for more. It's amazing how many people
never ask, and of the few who do, how few ever act on that precious advice. What fools! Just like Doug, I've met only one eager
student in my life. I am mentor to Mike Costache, a brilliant
young entrepreneur who is busy building a multimillion-dollar
company founded when he was only twenty-five years old. He
is the mirror image of me twenty years ago. Soon it will be Mike
earning millions, giving speeches, and writing books on success. His ultimate goal: to become ambassador to Romania. It
gives me great joy to know I helped mentor this superachiever.
But why do we meet only one eager student in a lifetime? *What
are the rest of you thinking?*

ROLE MODELS

I love to read about the lives of the superachievers who serve as
my personal role models. Their attitudes about success have inspired me every step of my journey. My first advice: Turn off
the "boob tube" and start reading the biographies of superachievers. A few of my favorites are Ronald Reagan, Winston
Churchill, George Washington, Abraham Lincoln, Benjamin
Franklin, General Robert E. Lee, General George S. Patton,
Sir William Wallace (otherwise known as "Braveheart"), the

Reverends Norman Vincent Peale, Billy Graham, and Robert Schuller, Oprah Winfrey, Golda Meir (the first female prime minister of Israel), John F. Kennedy, Senator John McCain, and great historical figures like Moses and Jesus Christ (as a Millionaire Republican, I enjoy books that apply Jesus' life and lessons to business, such as *Jesus CEO* and *The Leadership Lessons of Jesus*). I have read the biographies of every one of these superachievers and have learned more about life and success in the real world from their amazing stories than I ever learned from my Ivy League education. And just as important, their stories and successes—even though some of the ideas are many decades or centuries old—motivated me through tough times and inspired many of my best (and most profitable) ideas.

Along this same line, I recommend a daily barrage of self-help and motivational books, "books on tape," and audio series. We all need to be "pumped up" as often as possible. Life is difficult, complicated, and at times overwhelming. Self-help seminars, books, and audiotapes give us needed energy, inspiration, and pick-me-ups at just the right moments. Hearing or reading words of encouragement has often increased my creativity and inspired my best ideas. I've listened to hundreds of books on tape, as well as a historical tape series on greatness—the greatest composers of all time, the greatest literature, the greatest business leaders, the greatest military leaders, the greatest political leaders, the greatest religious leaders, etc. These tapes are available to anyone. By spending your driving time educating yourself about these great superachievers, you can get the equivalent of a college education (perhaps better) for pennies on the dollar. I won't deny that the sheepskin degree is a huge plus to open doors for your career (and for that reason alone can be worth every penny). But knowing what to do when the door is opened is even more important. And unfortunately, liberal educators don't choose to teach your children that at college. How foolish and shortsighted!

RESEARCH

Research doesn't mean going to the library. It means staying abreast of financial trends, current events, and what the top "red media" outlets and politicians are saying and doing. I recommend reading several newspapers and at least one financial publication each day. Years ago, I met my first $100 million business mogul. I was a young impressionable kid, and I listened and absorbed like a sponge. His most important advice was to read the *Wall Street Journal* every day and to pay special attention to the editorial page. This superachiever was a Republican (of course). He told me that the information, advice, and opinions I read in the *WSJ* would change my life. I followed his advice and have never regretted it. For the last twenty years I've been reading the *Wall Street Journal* (and studying the opinions on that editorial page). So should you. The wisdom found there will teach you to think like a Millionaire Republican. And as I've said again and again, you must think like a millionaire *before* you can become one!

But there's more to life than just the *WSJ*. I also read *Forbes*, *Fortune*, *Barron's*, *NewsMax*, and the *Robb Report* (the magazine of millionaires). During each business day, I keep my televisions tuned to CNBC (for business news) and FOX News Channel (for news and political talk). Why do I choose these specific media outlets? Plain and simple: These are the publications and TV networks that successful entrepreneurs and self-made millionaires read and watch.

I predict "new media" will dominate the future—just as it now dominates my daily routine. I now get much of my news and information online. I check in daily with FoxNews.com, NewsMax.com (my favorite political web site), DrudgeReport.com, CNBC.com, and of course my company's web site, WinningEDGE.com (for sports and gaming news and commentary direct from Wayne Allyn Root and my staff). By the time you're done educating yourself with all of the sources above, you will know more about news, business, politics, sales, religion—literally, more about *everything*—than anyone you do business with. And that, my friends, is how you become a Millionaire Republican! Let Democrats waste their time complaining, whining, attending protests, and screaming about how unfair life is. Meanwhile, Millionaire Republicans are focused on improving and *owning* our educations and personal growth, twenty-four hours a day, seven days a week. But we make sure we learn from the *right* role models and media—from other entrepreneurial thinkers and millionaires. That's how you get to be a rich Republican!

Secret # 10: Own *Your Political Future*

One person (at least in America) can make a difference! Your job as an aspiring Millionaire Republican is to fight for smaller, less intrusive government. The perfect examples of this theory at work are red states like Nevada, Arizona, Colorado, Utah, Texas, Florida, Idaho, etc. These are the states that made the top of the "Economic Freedom Index" that I reported on earlier. These are the states that lead the nation year after year in population growth, job growth, personal income growth, and small-business growth. These are also the states with the lowest taxes and smallest governments. Not coincidentally, these are also the states that consistently vote Republican red! Voting and supporting GOP candidates is the way to keep your red state in the black (financially). Less government intrusion and lower taxes equal more jobs, more success for small business and entrepreneurs, a more robust economy, and more freedom for you and your family.

What steps can you take to personally ensure that we keep moving in that direction? Vote Republican. Contribute to GOP causes and candidates who support lower taxes and smaller government. Show your true colors publicly through letters to the editor, phone calls, and letters to your congressman and other elected officials. Actively campaign for Republican candidates— it's good for your pocketbook, and the people you'll meet are fellow superachievers (the side bonus of actively working on behalf of GOP candidates is you get to network with other wealthy, successful Republicans, which could create major business opportunities). And contribute to GOP candidates until it hurts. It's one of the best investments you can ever make. In other words, take *action* to ensure a better financial future for you and your family, just as you do in the business world. Let me stress that the single most important thing you can do is contribute money. I've always said, "One liberal can join a protest march, or I can contribute enough money so that ten people can devote themselves full-time to the opposing cause!" I consider my donations to the Republican Party an *investment* in my future. I always take *action* and put my money where my mouth is when it comes to accumulating wealth, lowering my taxes, or fighting for candidates and causes in which I believe. That's why Millionaire Republicans always come out ahead!

Secret # 11: Own *More of Your Own Money*

This secret will be quick, short, and simple. It's not only the money you make that counts—it's the money you *keep.* I have explained again and again that attaining wealth is all about attitude. You must understand wealth and get comfortable with it *before* you can earn it. The same attitude applies to taxes. If you are going to keep more of your own money, you'll need to understand the way the game is played, think about ways to minimize your tax liability on a regular basis, and immerse yourself in financial and tax planning. You'll also need to hire the best accountant and estate and trust attorney you can find. Financial planning and cutting your taxes is not an afterthought on April 14. It is a full-time job. I think about it 364 days a year (I do take Christmas off). I save every tax-deductible receipt—and I do mean *every* one (down to the fifty cents I spend on a newspaper I read for business). I save every restaurant receipt, and include on it the date, place, amount, client, and detailed reason for the business meal. I am so organized and detail-oriented that even the IRS agents are impressed! I take my taxes very seriously. To me, it's a whole second side to business—making money is Part A; *keeping* my money by lowering my taxes is Part B.

I'd never cheat on my taxes. But I do everything within my legal power to keep my own money. I'm always amazed when I see people in old, inexpensive cars leaving a gas station without a gas receipt, or a restaurant without the meal receipt. I'm the only one I ever notice asking for the fifty-cent newspaper receipt at the newsstand. Why? Aren't the rest of you deducting the items you use for business? If you're not, you're a damn fool. Ironically, anyone who is driving an old piece-of-junk car needs to be thinking more seriously than me about how to lower their taxes. That's probably why they're driving that old clunker in the first place! It is your legal right to read every tax book, identify every legal deduction, and then go out and use them. (Democrats call them loopholes, but just as they don't understand wealth, liberals don't understand taxes either.) You must understand the importance of this pursuit: Every dollar you give to the IRS is a dollar you *won't* have for retirement, or your kid's college education, or buying your dream home, or taking your wedding anniversary cruise. It's *your* money. You'd guard it from thieves, wouldn't you? Why aren't you guarding it from the IRS? Their job is to do everything they legally can to take it from you. Your job is to do everything legally possible (armed with the latest information and knowledge) to stop them. I promise you that all Millionaire Republicans look at it that way. Do you?

Using the steps outlined above is the first step in lowering your taxes and keeping more of your own money. But simply thinking like a Millionaire Republican is the second step in lowering your taxes. By implementing the Republican secrets listed in this chapter, you'll automatically be lowering your tax liability. By living in a red state, you've lowered your tax bill. By owning stocks and real estate, you've lowered your tax bill (by paying only 15 percent capital gains tax). By selling your home (main residence) every two years, you've earned as much as $500,000 tax free. (If you're not taking advantage of this one, you're a damn fool!) By starting and owning your own business (even something as small and simple as a home-based business or MLM—multi-level marketing distributorship), you've lowered your tax bill by legally applying all your business expenses to your income. Since Republican politicians fight to keep taxes lower (especially for the self-employed and small-business owners), you automatically lower your tax bill by voting Republican and donating to GOP politicians. And then there are the tax fights you should be supporting: some form of Social Security privatization, a permanent end to death taxes, the implementation of a taxpayer Bill of Rights (TABOR) in your state to limit government spending, and a Prop 13–like amendment to limit the rise in local property taxes. Remember that your money is just that—*your money*. The purpose of this book is simple: As you start to think like a Millionaire Republican, you'll not only start to earn more money, you'll *keep* more of what you earn as well!

Secret # 12: Own the Baby Boom Generation

Millionaire Republicans will be investing in the aging population boom—if you're smart, so will you! There is no surprise here. America is growing older. *USA Today* recently reported that seniors will soon outnumber school-age children in many states! This "graying of America" just backs up much of what I've predicted in this book.

- Retirees are tax-conscious. Therefore, they are moving to Republican red states where income taxes and property taxes are lower.
- They are security-conscious. Therefore, they are choosing guard-gated communities in suburbs or exurbs (the fastest-growing regions for Republican voters).

- As people age, they tend to return to their religious roots. Therefore, they are returning to church in record numbers (and regular church attendees vote overwhelmingly Republican).

- Older Americans have more free time. One of the ways they are entertaining themselves is by gambling in Las Vegas and at tribal casinos in record numbers.

- They need a little extra money to enjoy their retirements in style. Therefore, they're working from home as independent contractors or opening small businesses. Studies show that older Americans are the fastest-growing segment starting small businesses.

- More older Americans will retire with savings and assets to protect. The result is that they will vote for politicians who want to reduce wasteful government spending and cut property taxes.

- More older Americans will retire to foreign tax havens. As discussed earlier, diversifying your investment portfolio by owning the right kind of foreign real estate is a great way to capitalize on this trend.

But the hottest trend of all is that older Americans are health-conscious and want to take care of their bodies. This means a big bet on *vanity*. This Millionaire Republican believes that companies that sell youth, beauty, and the healthy lifestyle will thrive. Cosmetic surgery is a great example. Everyone wants to look young, healthy, and sexy. Because of the success of a dozen plastic surgery/extreme makeover shows on television, plastic surgery is no longer considered a luxury solely for the super-wealthy. Americans are choosing to defy aging in record numbers. That's just one more reason to aim to become a Millionaire Republican—plastic surgery isn't cheap! Only those with disposable income can afford to look young and sexy (and therefore capitalize on that youthful look to make *more* money). Youth at any price, combined with a population explosion of older Americans with lots of disposable income, dictates investing in plastic surgery centers, cosmetic dentistry centers, preventative medicine clinics, antiaging centers, diet centers, day spas, companies that promote beauty and wellness, health food superstores (like Whole Foods Markets and Wild Oats), and companies that manufacture or distribute vitamins, organic food, fitness equipment (especially home gym products), and antiaging potions. You can bet that Millionaire Republicans will be opening small businesses that capitalize on this trend, and buying stocks of public companies that do too.

This Baby Boomer population explosion will drain government resources and entitlement programs (Social Security, Medicare, etc.), and thereby create tough times and tough choices—as *USA Today* recently put it, "[The Baby Boomer retirement explosion] promises to intensify the political tug-of-war between young and old for scarce resources." As usual, the masses of fearful, uneducated, and government-dependent Americans (called Democrats) will sit around and watch as America ages, governments strain, and our economy struggles—while visionary Millionaire Republicans will capitalize and profit on what may be the best investment opportunity of the twenty-first century!

Secret # 13: Own *Faith, Family, and Philanthropy*

Study after study proves that faith in God and prayer are good for you—mentally, physically, emotionally, and financially. A recent quote from the *Wall Street Journal* on the topic: "A growing body of scientific evidence shows that Americans who attend religious services at least once a week enjoy better-than-average health and lower rates of illness, including depression. Perhaps most important, the studies show that weekly attendance confers a ... 25% lower mortality rate." Studies also show that Americans who attend church regularly tend to vote *overwhelmingly* Republican. And married Americans tend to vote overwhelmingly Republican, too. (The media often talks about the "gender gap." But the fact is that married women vote Republican.) Traditional values may be a joke to Liberal Democrats, intellectuals, and the liberal media, but they sure seem to work in the real world!

Why do I think God and prayer help you to become healthier and wealthier? For me personally, prayer has always unleashed tremendous feelings of optimism, positive attitude, confidence, and creativity. In that way, I believe that prayer is the ultimate form of *positive thinking*. With the support of God, things you never dreamed you could accomplish on your own are suddenly within reach. Conversely, things that you couldn't deal with on your own are magically lifted off your shoulders through a faith in God. In either case, God is the ultimate partner. It can't be a coincidence that all that failing I told you about early in my career came during a period when I did not have God in my life and did not pray regularly. And the phenomenal success I have achieved since has all occurred *after* I developed a strong personal faith in God and prayer. God and my family are my rock and my foundation.

I don't know whether being married, attending religious services, and praying to God creates balance and success, or whether people who are balanced, successful, and wealthy just tend to be more positive people and credit God for their blessings. It really doesn't matter. The point is that Millionaire Republicans seem to get strength (and *financial* success) from a faith in God and prayer. That includes me. The more I pray, the more faith I exhibit. And the more faith I feel, the more confidence I exude and the more success I achieve. Quite simply, God is the greatest, most positive business partner I've ever met!

Let me make one last point on this subject. Liberals whine, complain, and protest (hand in hand with the ACLU) about God being too prevalent and violating the rights of nonbelievers. Well, the reality is that a huge majority of Americans want the right and freedom to worship, praise, and honor God wherever and whenever they wish. We have a right to pray or praise

God, just as liberals or atheists have the right not to. To prevent us from expressing our love for God is just as much a violation and abuse of our rights as my forcing an atheist to pray would be a violation of his rights.

In America, all of us are free to not believe in God, to not pray, and to not attend religious services. Amen—I appreciate those freedoms. But that won't stop me from presenting my opinion and telling you what has worked for me. It is my belief and experience that God is the secret weapon of successful Millionaire Republicans. Liberals are negative, cynical, bitter, and as a result, perennially see the glass as half empty. That could be the result of refusing to have faith, refusing to see prayer as helpful, refusing to believe that we all have a powerful (but unseen) partner by our side. On the other hand, I believe that because Republicans tend to be more religious, and because faithful people see things more cheerfully (always seeing the glass as half full), Republicans are automatically more positive and less fearful. And it is my experience that positive people do better in life than negative people. As such, Republicans are more likely to experience higher levels of health and wealth. Faith in God and prayer is just another secret weapon in the arsenal of Millionaire Republicans.

Part II of this secret is family—more specifically, traditional family values. Family goes hand in hand with faith. This one will really get the liberals howling: *I believe in traditional marriage* (a man and a woman committing together for life). I credit that institution for the financial security I have achieved—hand in hand with faith in God and prayer. But because I am an open-minded Libertarian Republican, I don't want to force my values on others. I want government out of our lives and bedrooms. I believe all Americans should be free to live our lives however we choose. But that doesn't mean I don't know a good thing when I see it, and the traditional marriage model works, *period!* Here's my definition of traditional: one parent "specializes" in earning money (a traditional CEO), and the other is the CEO of the household, "specializing" in taking care of the family and the needs of the household. I credit my financial success to that *specific* model. I am a workaholic—I think about business, run my company, write my books, produce my TV shows, and create new business ideas twenty-four hours a day. I am able to do all that because every other duty, responsibility, and worry is off my shoulders—my wife, Debra, takes on everything else. My plate is clean—my only job is to create wealth. Is that religious, square, or traditional? Maybe so, but it just plain works! That is how most Millionaire Republicans become millionaires. Behind most Millionaire Republicans is a spouse who makes all that success possible by taking all the other burdens off their shoulders. My wife is the greatest mother and CEO of the family I've ever seen. She's far better at running a family and household than I could ever be. I'm far better at making money than she could ever be. We make a great team. Today's obsession with "political correctness" is a massive failure. *Specialization* is what works best—each spouse specializes in either creating wealth or taking care of the family. Sometimes the old-fashioned, traditional way just happens to be the *right* way.

Finally we come to Part III of Faith, Family, and Philanthropy. Liberal Democrats see Millionaire Republicans as greedy. That couldn't be farther from the truth. Wealth is what allows us to give generously to charity and improve the world with the stroke of a pen (on our check). It is a *lack* of money that leaves individuals feeling helpless to right wrongs and help those in need. When Millionaire Republicans see an injustice, we can write a big fat check and provide an instant solution. Because of their lack of understanding about wealth, all Liberal Democrats can do is complain, whine, protest, cry, or write insignificant checks that change nothing. With all the liberal demagoguery and propaganda about "greedy Republicans," the truth is that individuals attaining wealth is better for *everyone*—including the poor and needy. A recent study reported in the *Wall Street Journal* proves my point. All twenty-five of the top twenty-five states that give most generously to charity (per capita) are *Republican red states that voted for George W. Bush.*

What factors would account for this remarkable statistical imbalance? Perhaps Republicans give more generously to charity because they are more religious and therefore feel more obligated to tithe to their churches and temples. Or perhaps liberals are hypocrites who talk a good game but never actually deliver. But most likely, it's as simple as the fact that Republicans earn substantially more money, so we have more to give!

We *own* instead of rent—and that gives us the wealth to create a better world. Who cares about the whys? In the end, Republicans give more to charity and make the world a better place— and that's *good*. I love to donate my money to help others. It makes me even more of a positive thinker. It makes me feel that I *deserve* to be successful. And I believe that what goes around comes around. The more I give, the more I seem to get! Is it the chicken or the egg? Do Millionaire Republicans give more money to charity because they are rich? Or do they become rich because they give generously to charity? As the famous movie line goes, Frankly, my dear, I don't give a damn. Every time I give, it seems to come back to me 100 times over. Charity is another important Millionaire Republican wealth-building secret.

Secret # 14: Own Your Own Body, Mind, and Spirit (with "Positive Addictions")

The word "addiction" is associated with bad habits, and rightfully so. Most people, when stressed, depressed, or just plain bored, turn to addictions like junk food, alcohol, cigarettes, drugs, or too much junk television—*all* damaging addictions. Millionaire Republicans, when faced with the same stresses, turn to "Positive Addictions"—exercise, prayer, meditation, visualization, healthy eating, and simply working harder. We get high *naturally*—on life.

You need no more evidence than to walk into any government unemployment, welfare, or mental health office. What do you see? You see grossly obese people stuffing their faces with junk food, cigarettes dangling from their mouths, saddled with alcohol and drug problems. The poorest Americans literally live on junk food and fast food: sugar-filled and preservative-laced crap that drains them of energy, health, mental balance, positive attitude, and focus. The facts are simple. The food you put into your body and the way you take care of your body are major factors in determining your level of wealth and success. Discipline, eating healthy, exercising, and avoiding smoking, alcohol, and drugs create a healthy body, mind, and spirit. You'll desperately need all of those to create the energy, enthusiasm, creativity, tenacity, and focus necessary to *thrive* in this highly competitive and stressful twenty-first-century work environment. Only the best of the best will reach the top. A majority (although certainly not all) of those winners at life will be mentally and physically fit.

There is no question that a disproportionate number of Millionaire Republicans tend to be married early risers who focus on staying fit and rely on a faith in God, prayer, and family. We are not partiers. We are not potheads. We don't hang out in nightclubs. We are not eating our meals at McDonald's. We just get up early, work hard and *religiously* for our families, come home to eat dinner with the entire family gathered around the table, and go to bed early to start it all over again tomorrow. It may sound boring and square, but it's darn effective for attaining wealth!

A study recently quoted in *USA Today* concluded that a typical individual's lifetime of smoking costs well over $3 million, counting the cost of cigarettes, sick days, doctor visits, higher health and life insurance payments, plus interest. The authors of that study did not look at alcohol or drugs, which are even bigger cash drains than smoking! So simply choosing not to smoke creates not only robust health and a longer life, but also a *wealthier* life. Think of the things you could do with an extra few million dollars. It really is this simple: Health equals wealth, and it is an important component of becoming a Millionaire Republican.

This New Age Republican (with a lot of old-fashioned values) starts every day with prayer, meditation, visualization, yoga, nature walks, aerobic exercise, weight and strength training, mega-vitamin supplementation, and an organic diet. This health regimen supercharges my body, mind, and spirit. It keeps me positive when things are not going according to plan. It keeps my energy, focus, and creativity high and allows me to work fourteen-hour days on multiple projects and multiple tasks. It keeps me healthy in the face of tremendous stress and high pressure that might debilitate lesser men or women. It keeps me thin and fit. It's pretty simple: If you're battling disease or illness, you don't have the strength to earn big bucks. As a matter of fact, you're probably spending all the money you do have on medical bills. You can't get rich without health. Along with God and family, healthy diet and lifestyle are the *foundations* of my life. Eating right, exercise, spiritual balance, and positive thinking all go hand in hand with the Millionaire Republican philosophy. By living your life with Positive Addictions instead of the negative addictions so prevalent among the poor and liberal complainers of this world, you can *own* versus rent your body, mind, spirit, and wallet!

For a more detailed look at my specific daily diet, health, and fitness recommedations, please refer to my book *The Zen of Gambling* (also a Tarcher/Penguin book), and in particular to the chapter titled "The Spiritual Gambler: Cultivating Positive Addictions."

Secret #15: Own *Your Decisions* and Disown *the Critics*

Up until now, my Millionaire Republican secrets have primarily outlined ways to think, act, and invest to capitalize on the Republican Red Storm upon us. These last four secrets are a bit different. These are *secret ingredients* necessary to ensure you have the chutzpah (or balls, as we say in New York) to implement the Millionaire Republican secrets.

First and foremost, Millionaire Republicans are decisive and confident. We believe in ourselves and our decisions. We may be big dreamers and big risk-takers, but we are willing to put our money where our mouths are. We are willing to take *ownership* of our decisions (right or wrong) and the risks that go along with them. We're willing to back up our opinions by putting our assets on the line, instead of collecting a "safe" paycheck and second-guessing others from the sidelines. Hand in hand with our strength of character and commitment is an understanding that critics are *idiots.* I've always said of critics, "Those who can, do; those who can't, criticize. And those who can't do anything at all, criticize for a living in the media." But it's not just the media critics you've got to ignore. Critics are often your own friends and family. Critics all have the same effect—they destroy your dreams. They create doubt, deflate your spirit, and weaken your energy. They often stop you dead in your tracks.

President George W. Bush has been mercilessly criticized for being too headstrong, for being too committed to his plans, and for a willingness to take big risks (huge tax cuts, the war in Iraq, privatizing Social Security). But that's precisely what a leader does! Only a weak-willed liberal who settles for a "safe" job, collects a guaranteed paycheck, has no backbone for risk, and rarely is given the authority to make a tough decision would dare criticize a decisive leader willing to take daring risks to make the world a better place. With this criticism, liberals show they simply don't have what it takes to be leaders. Why do you suppose John Kerry was known for his flip-flops on the issues? Because he didn't have the intestinal fortitude to stand up and be a strong leader. Or, worse yet, his only opinions were what the public opinion polls told him to believe. It is said you either stand for something or you stand for nothing. Liberals stand for nothing—except criticizing.

Critics do not produce anything—not goods, not ideas, not

jobs. *Nothing.* They wait for others to take action, then criticize the results. To criticize contributes nothing to a society. On the other hand, a willingness to risk by taking action is at the center of all that is creative, positive, and groundbreaking. This willingness to risk literally defines Millionaire Republicans. They are the doers, achievers, explorers, and thrivers of our world. And a successful risk-taker is by definition a dedicated contrarian. Risk-takers are willing to do, create, explore, discover, invent, or achieve what critics say *cannot* be done. Risk is essential to success. To take those risks and make the tough decisions, you'll need to learn to trust your own instincts, to *own* your decisions, and to *disown* the critics.

Over the years I've compiled examples of many critics and so-called experts who were proven wrong (*badly* wrong) and the remarkable, often magical results achieved by those who ignored them. I appreciate and thank all those whose research and tenacity uncovered such priceless sources of motivation. Here are a few of my favorite quotes of all time, proving beyond a shadow of a doubt that critics are idiots.

- **1929: "Stocks have reached what looks like a permanently high plateau."**

    Who said it? Irving Fischer, America's leading economist, only nine days before the great stock market crash of 1929! Irving was the first in a long line of economists whose predictions never fail to make us laugh (and make us broke).

- **1911: "Airplanes are interesting toys but of no military value."**

  Who said it? Marshal Ferdinand, Commander of French military forces in World War I. Since then it has been French military forces that have proven to be of no military value!

- **1876: "This device has too many shortcomings to be seriously considered as a means of communication. This device is inherently of no value to us."**

  Who said it? Unnamed executives at Western Union, talking about the telephone! But we all know the name of the risk-taker who invented the telephone: Alexander Graham Bell! Throughout history, critics have always been forgotten.

- **1977: "There is no reason why anyone would want a computer in their home."**

  Who said it? Ken Olsen, founder of the Digital Equipment Corporation, at a meeting of the World Future Society. See what I mean about "experts"? The World Future Society? I wonder if Mr. Olsen and his fellow experts also missed the value of indoor plumbing.

- **1967: "Man will never reach the moon . . . regardless of all future scientific advances."**

  Who said it? Dr. Lee DeForester, a respected scientist and the father of radio. Note the date. Not only are experts often *pompous fools,* but they also usually make their absurd predictions only a short time before being proven wrong (and stupid).

- **1957: "The Edsel is here to stay."**

  Who said it? Henry Ford, founder of Ford Motor Company. Soon after that brilliant quote, the Edsel went the way of . . . the Edsel!

- **1920: "The wireless box has no commercial value. Who would pay for a message sent to nobody in particular?"**

  Who said it? A communications expert, talking about the radio, to David Sarnoff. Radio has more than held its own since 1920, wouldn't you say? And thanks to the current success of satellite radio, we now know that listeners are willing to pay a monthly fee for a message sent to nobody in particular!

- **1972: "The current craze for bottled water is 'lunatic asylum thinking.' It will fade away as quickly as it came."**

  Who said it? Dr. Abel Wolman, professor at Johns Hopkins University, known as America's leading authority on water! After selling the stocks of Evian and Perrier short, my guess is poor Professor Wolman didn't have enough money left to buy a bottle of water!

- **1955: "TV can never become truly popular. Who would stare at that 'boob tube' for hours on end?"**

  Who said it? A radio executive dismissing any chance for TV to overtake radio. First we read of telegraph "experts" panning the telephone. Then communication "experts" panning the radio. Now radio "experts" dismissing TV. See a pattern emerging here? Experts are *idiots.*

- **1965: "This concept is interesting but not feasible. A concept must be feasible to earn better than a C."**

  Who said it? A Yale economics professor commenting on college student Fred Smith's idea for an overnight delivery service to compete with the U.S. Postal Service. Smith went on to found Federal Express. FedEx today employs more than 200,000 people, serves 211 countries, and has annual revenues of over $20 billion! Today, many of us in the business world wonder whether the U.S. Postal Service can continue to compete with FedEx!

- **1989: "Test audiences hate this television pilot. They call it weak. They report that both the main characters and the supporting cast are unlikable. The humor is far 'too New York and Jewish.' The show rated as only mildly amusing. No segment of the audience was eager to ever watch the show again."**

  Who said it? Television "consultants" for NBC, reporting on the reaction by focus groups to *Seinfeld*—one of the most popular shows in TV history. More than fifty million viewers watched the last episode of *Seinfeld* in 1999, during which a thirty-second commercial cost $2 million! (Consultants are another form of idiots.)

- **1940: "The United States will not be a threat to us for decades, at the earliest 1970 or 1980."**

Who said that in 1940? *Adolf Hitler.* Luckily for the human race, this madman was off by over a quarter century!

- **1899: "Everything that can be invented has already been invented."**

    Who said it? The United States Commissioner of Patents *in 1899.* I saved the best for last! This has to be the single dumbest thing ever said by anyone ever. As I've always said, governments are stocked full of idiots who couldn't hold a job in the private sector!

Why do I quote these "experts" and big shots? Because these in-famous predictions prove my point: Listening to critics (even sup-posed "experts" in their field) will *ruin* your life. To become a Millionaire Republican, you must be independent-minded. You must be a leader willing to make decisions and stand by those deci-sions. You must be someone who doesn't follow rules, but makes them or *breaks* them! You must be someone who doesn't fold at the first sign of adversity, but instead stays committed in the face of bad news, bad luck, vicious criticism, or impossible odds. Does that remind you of anyone? *It is the very definition of President George W. Bush!* To be a political leader, business leader or owner, sales leader, corporate executive, entrepreneur, or Millionaire Republican of any kind, you must be a fearless decision maker and be willing to own your decisions and disown the critics!

Secret #16: Own *a Healthy Ego*

This Millionaire Republican secret goes hand in hand with owning your own decisions and disowning the critics. I call this secret "The Ego Rules!" It's pretty simple. Forget all the nonsense you are taught in school or self-help books about teamwork. It's a load of crap! Teamwork leads to a dead-end job and a "safe" paycheck. It's *ego* that gets you a million-dollar mansion and a Mercedes in the driveway. A healthy ego is the essential secret ingredient for any Millionaire Republican. Ego is what creates wealth, fame and power. Ego is good! More than good, ego is a *crucial* component of leadership. You don't become a millionaire CEO, a sales superstar, or build a chain of restaurants by being a wallflower. You must be forceful, action-oriented, aggressive, decisive, and confident. And yes, that requires a strong ego! Business leaders—CEOs, business owners, entrepreneurs, star salespersons—are often referred to as "rainmakers." They are the evangelists of the business world. They raise their hands and make the rains flow. Eventually the rains turn to torrents, then floods. These stars of the business world are swashbuckling *superheroes* with unlimited faith in their own ability to conquer new frontiers and overcome insurmountable obstacles. That doesn't mean these rainmakers or millionaires are arrogant. But it does mean they are confident, trust their instincts, and have the chutzpah to make decisions (often unpopular) and the committment to stick with them (or change them the moment they have better information).

Liberal do-gooders, psychologists, teachers, professors and assorted authors, speakers, and media experts constantly pound home the idea that ego is bad. Well, it may be bad for employees in "safe" jobs, who are paid a mediocre paycheck to follow orders. These are the people brainwashed into believing in their own powerlessness and lack of importance. If you want to be an order-taker your whole life, then by all means give up your ego and think only of "the team." In a big bureaucracy, it's true that you are just an easily replaced cog in a big wheel. But if your goal is to truly succeed—to achieve mega-wealth, to thrive, to own—then you had better understand that *ego rules.*

All leaders have ego, whether they are the CEO of IBM, GE, or Microsoft, the head coach of the Dallas Cowboys (yes, Bill Parcells definitely has a big ego), or the CEO of the corner Texaco station or local Chinese restaurant. For a leader, there are decisions to be made twenty-four hours a day, seven days a week, and you need a healthy ego to make them, and then to face the critics after the fact. Friends, relatives, employees, and consultants will all give you bad advice—you'll need a healthy ego to disregard it. I ran into a neighbor and friend the other day, a famous motivational speaker who has had books and movies written about his life. He commented to me that the key to his success is that he no longer asks anyone for advice— because whenever he did in the past, the advice was virtually always *wrong.* "If I had listened to people, I'd have never done any of the things that have made me wealthy and famous." Great advice!

But most of all, you'll need a healthy ego just to get into a position of power and leadership in the first place! Without a healthy ego, you'd never leave your "safe" job to strike out on your own. Without a healthy ego, you'd never go into sales (remember, that's where all the money is). Without a healthy ego, no salesperson could make hundreds of calls a day, facing rejection, failure, negativity, and even anger. Without ego, you'd never stake your home and assets on the line to guarantee a bank loan to fund your business. Without ego you'd never be willing to accept the stress and responsibilities of an entrepreneur, executive, CEO, or business owner.

I've been in sales my whole life (usually the product was me), and I've met many super salespeople. To succeed at selling yourself, your products, or your business, you'll need to become CEO of the most important business in the world—*Me, Inc.* You'll need to understand that the rules for entrepreneurs, business owners, executives, independent contractors, and performance-based salespeople are completely different than those for employees with that dreaded "safe" job and guaranteed paycheck. People who follow orders need to keep their egos in check. But to thrive in the dog-eat-dog business and sales world (where all the money is), you need to throw out everything you've ever learned in school about ego. Teamwork is for renters. *Ego is what creates ownership!* The problem is that our society, educational system, media, and employment system are set up all wrong (by liberals). They only teach you how to be an employee, follower, mindless order-taker, or renter. They don't teach you how to make decisions and take independent action. This is an archaic mind-set that meets with abysmal failure in the business, entrepreneurial, and sales worlds.

What does it take to succeed and attain wealth in sales or business? The *opposite* of all the traits and habits that are taught to you in school! You've got to be bold, assertive, aggressive, creative, independent (contrarian), confident, and action-oriented. You've got to learn to become a world-class salesperson and a shameless self-promoter. And of course, to pull all this off you've got to have a healthy ego. A recent Gallup poll reported that seven out of ten American high school students want to start their own businesses. Well, if that's so, they had better quickly *unlearn* everything they've ever learned in school about success! Kids with the kind of traits I'm recommending are often scolded and punished at school. Liberals want our kids to all get along, to give up their competitive nature, and to sing "Kumbaya" and "We Are the World." That's great if you want to graduate to a life of safety, security, and mediocrity—to a job with a boss you hate, that pays you enough to barely afford the rent on a studio apartment with a view of a wall, and a shiny new Saturn to go with it!

But if you want to succeed in the business world and become a millionaire, this "old school" curriculum is an albatross around your neck. By following the liberal rules taught in most schools and colleges, you've lost before the battle even begins. With the crap taught in school, you wouldn't last a week in sales and you certainly would never start your own business (that makes sales seem *easy* by comparison)! But the thrivers, superstars, rainmakers, and Millionaire Republicans of the sales and business world understand that it all comes down to ego—either you believe 100 percent in you, or no one else will. Besides, it ain't bragging if you can back it up!

Liberals will point to egotistical CEOs like Dennis Koz-lowski, Ken Lay, Jeff Skillings, John Rigas, and Bernie Ebbers to prove that ego is bad. I disagree. It wasn't ego that brought these men down. It was a lack of ethics. Ego combined with a lack of ethics equals arrogance, and *that* is a bad trait. Ego is what em-powers you to reach the top levels of power and success. What you do once you get there is up to you. But if you want even a shot at becoming a Millionaire Republican, you had better un-derstand that *ego rules.*

Secret #17: Own *Your Own Failures*

Here's another secret you're not taught in school. It's some-thing the vast masses of Americans have never quite grasped. To succeed, you must first get comfortable with failure and re-jection. I call it the *Joy of Failure.* All self-made Millionaire Republicans have experienced and learned from failure—usually numerous failures! Failure is just a natural part of the success journey. If you are going to be a courageous, daring, risk-taking entrepreneur, please understand before you start that *you will face failure.* You must be prepared to be rejected. You must be prepared to strike out. (I do it every day.) To become a Millionaire Republican, you must understand that with each failure or rejection, you are one step closer to achieving your goals and dreams. The people who never master success make a common fatal mistake: They focus on the failure and let it destroy their confidence, faith, and hope. They then hide from failure by never trying or risking again. Unfortunately, they learned the wrong lesson (remember my dad?).

Millionaire Republicans learn from the failure, block it out forever more, and move on. They attack the next challenge (or the same one over again) with the same positive attitude, passion, and gusto that they exhibited the last time. That could be why most if not all Millionaire Republicans are in sales. All the big money is in selling something. Yet sales revolves around *rejection* (often multiple times a day). Unless you were born with a trust fund, there is no other way to succeed but to risk, to be rejected, to fail again and again, to learn from those failures, and to get back up and sell again! Take it from me—if you choose to become a Millionaire Republican, the failure/rejection cycle will never end. As long as you are attacking aggressively and aiming high, there *will* be challenges, setbacks, and bad days. But by facing those negatives and staying in the game, you will find that one *yes* erases all the *no*'s. That's the mantra of Millionaire Republicans: One *yes* changes your life!

In the end, that is the secret that separated me from my father. He hated the no's. He despised the failures and rejections. He couldn't deal with pressure and stress. I hate the no's too, but they don't slow me down or make me doubt myself, my vision, or my decisions. I understand that each rejection or failure puts me that much closer to that magical yes that will change my life. I crave that yes so strongly, so clearly, so enthusiastically, that the yes is all I can see. That tunnel vision gives me the confidence I need to stay committed to my vision. The failures and setbacks along the way are meaningless (except as learning tools). *The yes is what I live for!* The *yes* is what all Millionaire Republicans live for. It's why we risk again and again. It's why we fight with such abandon and intensity. It's why we work late while others are watching the World Series and the Academy Awards. It's why we work nights, weekends, and holidays (which happens to be precisely when I found the time to write this book). It's why we persist in the face of endless critics, naysayers, and doomsdayers. It gives us energy when others have long since given up. *Yes* is the magic word. Fighting through countless failures for that one empowering *yes* is the magical secret ingredient that drives all Millionaire Republicans.

Just like your faith in God and the power of prayer, a faith in your talent and dreams is nothing more than the most perfect expression of positive thinking. Faith is believing 100 percent in something you can't touch or see but that you know with all your heart is there! Perhaps that's why Millionaire Republicans thrive. We understand faith. Our belief in God, despite a lack of scientific proof, also trains us to believe in ourselves, our dreams, and our ultimate success, even *before* we ever achieve them. We are *relentlessly* positive. We can clearly see the American Dream, when liberals see nothing but inequality, unfairness, prejudice, and lack of opportunity. We see the roots of success where liberals see only failure. We see one hundred rejections as a learning experience and still retain our faith that the next sales pitch or business idea will make us a millionaire. Liberals give up after the first rejection or sign of resistance.

Because this is how liberals think, they head off on a tangent for months of protest, complaining, soul-searching, and depression. What a sad way to live life. You're DOA with that attitude. You're lost in a world of antidepressants and psychologists. Millionaire Republicans have tunnel vision, too, but it's only the *positive* that we choose to see. Faith and optimism are our rock, our foundation. Faith is what empowers us to stand tall in the face of failure, rejection, and critics, to stay committed when all others have long since deserted the ship. We never stop thinking of that *yes.* We never lose sight of our goals and dreams. We never lose sight of that one *yes* that will change our lives. Our faith in God trains us to be faithful to our dreams as well.

And that, boys and girls, is precisely how you become a millionaire!

Secret #18: Own *It All (with* Passion*)*

This concept is so simple and elementary that it shouldn't even need to be mentioned. But it does. It's actually a two-parter. Part 1 is, as Nike would say, *just do it.* Show up and get the job done. Republicans get ahead because they are willing to get up every day and go to work. They take *personal responsibility* and do not complain, whine, or blame others. They are not allergic to hard work. They understand that success takes patience (running your own business often takes *extreme* hours—but it's yours, you own it, and the sacrifice is therefore worth it). The American Dream does not happen overnight. Sometimes achieving wealth takes decades, sometimes it takes more than one generation. Republicans do not lie on the couch watching Jerry Springer (a future Democrat politician, by the way) or soap operas, or seek out personal injury lawyers (the kind that usually advertise during Jerry Springer and soap operas) as their personal lottery payoffs. They do not waste their time seeing disaster, tragedy, prejudice, and injustice around every bend. They have a single-minded focus—I call it *Republican Tunnel Vision*—which looks only toward creating wealth and improving their lives and the lives of their families. They don't spend a lot of time talking about it, or wasting their time being jealous of others, *they just do it.* The irony is that if Democratic voters dependent on government or stuck in low-wage jobs simply adopted a Millionaire Republican mind-set instead of wasting their time complaining, protesting, and focusing on perceived injustice and prejudice, they'd stand a good chance of becoming Millionaire Republicans. Then, of course, they'd have nothing to complain about!

Success is all about (ironically) what you can and cannot afford. You can't afford to whine and complain. You can't afford drugs, alcohol, or other negative addictions. You can't afford to be sick (people with positive attitudes have been shown to be much healthier than those with negative attitudes). You can't afford to take your eye off the ball for a second. Let others call in sick, or take weekends off, or demand higher pay for overtime, or just show up and bide their time until their pensions kick in, or join unions—*none of them will ever become Millionaire Republicans.* Success is such a delicate and complex process, you can't afford the distractions. You can't afford to waste a minute thinking about anything but building wealth 24/7. That's the final Millionaire Republican secret. There's no magic—that's the simple way you turn dreams into reality. Just do it—with *Republican Tunnel Vision.*

Part 2 of this last Republican secret is that whatever you do, do it with *passion.* While showing up and getting the job done is a good start, it's not enough. Millionaire Republicans are always passionate about their goals, their game plans, their products (usually themselves), and their chosen careers. You'll need that passion every step of the way.

What's the best way to maintain a passion for what you do? Find something that you love to do. Something that you were born to do. Something that *is* you. It is no coincidence that I failed early and often at the start of my career—but none of those jobs or business ventures was me. I wasn't passionate about anything I was doing, so I lacked committment. I never gave 180 percent. I didn't own it. All the careers and businesses where I've succeeded beyond my wildest dreams have been my *passions*—hosting television shows, making predictions, talking gambling, publishing (writing books about my passions), and now talking politics. These are the loves of my life. These are the things I was born to do. You cannot succeed unless you find that one thing that defines you, that one thing that fills you with passion. And once you find that one thing, you must *own it.*

Everything I do, I do with passion and abandon. I own it all! So must you. If the goal is sales, pick up that phone fearlessly, 200 times a day. If the goal is finding a spouse, take a personals ad or join an online dating service (anything you do, do it big). If the goal is making money by buying real estate, go out on a limb by buying the biggest home, with the biggest mortgage, in the best neighborhood, with the smallest down payment—stretch until you're ready to *burst.* If you're going to self-promote, model yourself after P. T. Barnum, the most shameless, passionate, and *successful* self-promoter ever. If you want to become a lawyer, model yourself after lawyers like Gloria Allred, Gerry Spence, or Alan Dershowitz (all liberals, by the way, but they're my kind of liberals: *passionate* ones)—committed, flamboyant lawyers who literally own their cases. They have tunnel vision—a single-minded determination to win.

Own whatever you do and you'll end up in the winner's circle, too!

My Parting Advice

Don't let anyone or anything stop you, slow you, or dissuade you. Don't let a day go by where you feel regret (for not giving 180 percent) or guilt (for pushing too hard). Don't worry about who you are bothering—successful salesmanship is all about bothering! Don't worry if everyone calls you a dreamer and says you've set your goals too high. All Millionaire Republicans aim for the stars. Don't worry if your ego offends someone—it will! And for God's sake, don't wait for anyone's permission. You cannot succeed by being polite or humble, or waiting for the permission of others—you'll be waiting until you're dead.

Most important, understand that there's a *yes* out there with your name on it—a *yes* that has the power to change your life. Keep the faith. Stay positive. Stay committed. Own your decisions. Own the risks necessary to strike it big and strike it rich. Own your failures (and learn from them). Own your ego. Own your passion. ***Own it all!*** Then go after your goals with such passion, intensity, energy, and abandon that you either succeed or *explode*. Search out opportunity like a heat-seeking missile. When you find it (or create it), kick its door down, seize it by the throat, knock it unconscious, and drag it home like a caveman (or cavewoman). That's how you own your job, your life, your future. *That's how you own it all.* That's how you become your own, card-carrying Millionaire Republican. I hope you have enjoyed your Extreme Republican Makeover! Now it's time to apply the 18 Republican Secrets of Mega-Wealth and Unlimited Success.

Good luck, God bless, and happy hunting!

Whatever you do, own it! Own it all!

—WAYNE ALLYN ROOT

Acknowledgments

Let me begin at the place where it all started for my family—Ellis Island. My grandparents Simon and Meta Reis left Germany in the early 1900s to travel to a strange land called America that they knew nothing about, without any money, friends, or family waiting on the other end. I often describe Republicans as America's backbone—courageous, daring, and bold entrepreneurial risk-takers. Well, if that's true, Simon and Meta Reis were the first Republicans. They defined "chutzpah" (Yiddish for "balls")! After first working as a butcher for twenty years, my grandfather started his own butcher store. By the time I came along in 1961, he was a successful small-business owner and a devoted Republican butcher! On the day I was born, my father worked in that little butcher store. That's where this book begins. Without the amazing courage and risks taken by my grandparents, I would not be a Millionaire Republican, nor an author writing about it. Thank you, Simon and Meta, for all you did. Thank you, Simon, for instilling in me my love of entrepreneurship and salesmanship. It's amazing to think that it all started in a small butcher store called Pondfield Market in Bronxville, New York. God, I love this country!

As you read this book, you'll find that my father, David Root, the Republican butcher from the mean streets of Brownsville, Brooklyn, was my biggest influence. He taught me the "Republican Rules" from almost the day I was born—*literally.* He had me handing out campaign literature for Barry Goldwater at the age of three! But most important, he believed in me. He made me believe in myself. He said from my earliest childhood memories that I'd graduate from Columbia University—and I did! He promised I'd become a millionaire if I followed the rules and values of the Republican Party—and I did! He promised I'd become a Republican United States senator one day—and I'm working on that goal right now. I know that as I wrote this book, my parents, David and Stella, were looking down from heaven with pride! I miss you both and still feel your love on a daily basis. I thought of you every day as I wrote this book. Thank you for the greatest gift of all—the foundation in life that created this Millionaire Republican.

Next I must acknowledge my present-day family—without their love and support I'd surely be lost. Let me start with my wife, Debra. Talk about blessings! She is a stunningly beautiful and statuesque blond goddess who can beat anyone at *Jeopardy!* She is college educated, with a master's and a Ph.D. in homeopathy, the science of healthy living and holistic medicine. She's a former Miss Oklahoma who speaks five languages. And a former lead singer for music legends like Ginger Baker and Emerson, Lake & Palmer. Too good to be true? I'm just getting warmed up! She's a gourmet cook and a spiritual dynamo who comes from a family of devoted, selfless Christian ministers and missionaries. Many men say that their wife is the perfect wife and mother. *Debra really is.* She gave up all the beauty contests, stadiums full of music fans, a promising acting career, and a successful business career to be Mrs. Wayne Root. To be my rock. To be the mother of Dakota, Hudson, and Remington. To serve as CEO of the Root household. That leaves me free to be me—to host and produce my TV shows, run my businesses, write my books, debate politics, and build my business empire. Thank God for Debra Root—she is the ultimate blessing!

Then there are our amazing children. My daughter, Dakota Skye Root, is the most beautiful, brilliant, and perfect child on this earth. I swear I'm not biased—if you knew her, you'd think the same thing! At the age of thirteen she scored *post* high school in virtually every category on the Stanford Achievement Tests. She reads as many as a dozen books a week; can outtalk and outdebate her father (a pretty fair debater); she's beautiful like her mother; and excels at martial arts, tennis, swimming, and fencing. My prediction is that Dakota's future includes a Miss USA title; a championship fencing career at Stanford University; and a political career far surpassing her father's. But Dakota is not the only special Root. Five-year-old Hudson Franklin Reis Root is a macho daddy's boy who loves playing and watching football, soccer, boxing, karate, and car racing with his father. He's been walking two miles with Dad every morning since the age of three. That morning walk is the joy of my life. I bound out of bed just to see Hudson every morning! And finally there's Remington Reagan Root (named after my hero, President Ronald Reagan). He's only ten months old as I write this. Like his namesake, he came out of the womb shaking hands like a politician (his hand literally ripped through Debra's cervix, the very week of President Reagan's funeral. Boy, does Remington Reagan understand timing! I have a feeling God has special things in store for my youngest child. Dakota, Hudson, and Remington Reagan are the lights of my life. They are the reason I work so hard—to ensure their future happiness and prosperity. Family is at the core of the success of all Millionaire Republicans.

Speaking of family—Douglas Miller is at the top of any list: best friend, mentor, loyal business partner. He was the first adult who ever believed in me and my talents. Without his counsel, advice, and wisdom, I could not and would not be where I am today. There would be no *Millionaire Republican.* Today he is COO and president of my company, GWIN Inc. He "watches the store" and runs the day-to-day operations of my business while I'm off writing books, hosting TV shows, giving speeches, handicapping winners, meeting and greeting fans and clients. He even edited the words you have just read in this book. I thank God for putting Doug in my life. Another in a series of miracles and blessings. Doug, like Debra, makes it easy for me to be Wayne!

Other family members who must be acknowledged: Ralph

and Martha Parks (Debra's mom and dad), who after the death of my parents literally just took over as my mom and dad. They are the reason Debra is a world-class wife and mother. They recently moved to Las Vegas to be in their grandchildren's lives on a daily basis. If my life sounds like a fairy tale, it is, and the Parks family is the reason why! Many people talk about God and spirituality—the Parks family *lives* it. Thanks also to my sister, Lori Brown, and her husband, Doug; and my siblings-in-law Minister Charlie and Darla Finnochiaro.

Now to a few business acknowledgments. First there are my senior editors at Penguin Group USA, Joel Fotinos and Mitch Horowitz. This book was rushed and released only through the herculean efforts of Joel, Mitch, and my line-by-line editor, Terri Hennessy—I'm forever grateful for your professionalism, work ethic, and teamwork. Then there are the public-relations efforts of Ken Siman. Ken is the best in the publishing business. Without publicity and promotion, there are no book sales! Penguin also published my last book, *The Zen of Gambling*. It has been an honor working with all of the professionals at Penguin over the last two years and multiple books. The execs at Penguin may not realize it (yet), but you're all world-class Millionaire Republicans! You see, the very traits that define Republican businesspeople are courage, daring, chutzpah, vision, and a willingness to take risks. Who else would have had the chutzpah and vision to allow the world's most famous gambler to write a book about Republican politics?

To my team at GWIN Inc., so many of you run the business

so that I can receive the glory—Jeff Johnson (my CFO), Hollis Barnhart (my general manager), Rocky Attolico (sales manager), John McIntire (operations manager), and Kevin Mott (living proof that New Yorkers excel at salesmanship), to name just a few. Hollis in particular has been by my side in one capacity or another for almost fifteen years. He is like a brother to me. Without friends like Hollis, business would just be work.

Other key players at Team Root who must be acknowledged: my attorney, Lee Sacks—a true spiritual warrior on my behalf (and the best darned lawyer in the entertainment business). Like Hollis and Doug Miller, Lee is another business associate who has grown into beloved friend and family member. Michael Yudin, who first believed in my TV talents almost twenty years ago and today is my executive producer partner for our *King of Vegas* series on Spike TV. Michael introduced me to all the people at Spike TV who will ensure that *King of Vegas* is a big success—special thanks to Doug Herzog, Kevin Kay, and Brian Gadinsky. Roger Harrison, one of the nicest and most loyal men I have ever met, today serves not only as a valued member of the GWIN board of directors but as "Uncle Roger" to my children. Matt Brooks, the National Executive Director of the Republican Jewish Coalition, has been a loyal friend and counsel to me in all my political pursuits. Petar Lasic, my first videographer and friend in the television business at Financial News Network, has served as the director of all of my TV shows ever since. Arnie Rosenthal deserves special thanks—he was the first television executive to see the spark in me and he took a huge chance on a young, raw talent. I will be forever grateful to you, Arnie, for having the vision to see what others could not. Doug Fleming, my high school principal back in New Rochelle, New York, twenty-five years ago. Doug and I have a truly unique relationship—how many students count their principal as a close friend a quarter-century later? People often talk about a favorite educator. In my lifetime, that one favorite educator who made such a difference in my life was Doug Fleming. It was only through Doug's efforts, guidance, and persistence that I was accepted into Columbia University. And finally, a few friends without whom I just wouldn't be the same person: Matt Schiff, Carl Cohen, Steve Richman, Monte Weiner, Jeff Postal, Jerry Goldman, J. C. Long, Steve Pashalis, Jimmy and Dean Doukas, John Manner, Bruce Merrin, and Wilson Rondini. I count all of you as valued and trusted friends—and you have all been invaluable in building my career, business, and life.

On the political front, I want to thank my hero, President Ronald Reagan. Reagan was president while I was attending Columbia University and throughout my early years as an aspiring entrepreneur. I never met Ronald Reagan, yet I always thought of him as a second father. Even now, I think of him often. I will always be a Ronald Reagan Republican. I also want to thank President George W. Bush, who has displayed the same courage, commitment, and values that Reagan did—and the same fervor for unabashedly cutting taxes for the small businesspersons and daring entrepreneurs who create all the jobs, growth, and prosperity for this great country. I consider it an honor and great omen that "W" was serving as our president as I wrote *Millionaire Republican.*

I'd be remiss not to acknowledge my critics. No statue has ever been built to honor a critic. You are the people who achieve, accomplish, and create absolutely nothing. (It's no coincidence that most critics are liberals.) You have the easiest job in the world—you just sit back and criticize and insult what others have built. But you do serve a purpose: You have inspired my success every step of the way. To all of you who didn't see the spark, didn't recognize my potential, never acknowledged my talents, criticized me or underestimated me—you are the very ones who motivated me to overachieve. It is you who produced my energy, enthusiasm, passion, commitment, tenacity, fire, drive, and determination. It was your inspiration that led to this *Millionaire Republican* book. Thank you. I owe you a debt of gratitude.

Finally, this book is dedicated to God. God inspired every word that I put to paper in *Millionaire Republican.* Everything I do, everything I achieve, everything I am, it's all because of God, and dedicated to God. I thank God for all the blessings He has bestowed upon me—but especially for all the family and friends named above! It is those relationships that make me wealthy. This Millionaire Republican has been truly blessed. I hope and pray that each of you reading this book is equally blessed. I pray that this book transforms lives and inspires a new generation of Millionaire Republicans. I hope you're one of them! God bless.

A Few Parting Words

This doesn't have to be an ending. It can be a beginning. I'm excited and committed to changing this world—one Millionaire Republican at a time. I'd love to hear from you! Please e-mail me or write with your comments, requests, or questions. Visit my website at www.MillionaireRepublican.com or at www.WayneRoot.com, or e-mail me directly at war@millionairerepublican.com.

For information on my other books, videos, audiotapes, or my availability for speeches and seminars anywhere in the world, please visit my website at www.MillionaireRepublican.com.

Or contact:
Wayne Allyn Root
Millionaire Republican Inc.
2505 Anthem Village Drive, Suite E 318
Henderson, Nevada 89052
Phone: (702) 407–5548
Fax: (702) 407–5188

About the Author

Wayne Allyn Root is a popular author, TV and radio host, entrepreneur extraordinaire, and one of America's leading professional strategists and soothsayers. He is the star of *Wayne Allyn Root's WinningEDGE™* on Superstation WGN, host of the *WinningEDGE* radio show, heard on major sports stations around the country, and CEO of GWIN Inc., America's only publicly traded sports handicapping company. He stars in and executive produces the forthcoming Spike TV show *King of Vegas,* a national competition to crown the greatest gambler in America. Root lives in Las Vegas, Nevada (a red state), with his wife and their three children.